DR. FULFORD'S
Touch of Life

DR. FULFORD'S
Touch of Life

*The Healing Power
of the Natural Life Force*

Robert C. Fulford, D.O.
with Gene Stone

POCKET BOOKS
New York   London   Toronto   Sydney   Tokyo   Singapore

The ideas, procedures and suggestions in this book are not intended to sub-stitute for the personal advice of your trained health professional. All mat-ters regarding your health require medical supervision. You may wish to consult your physician before adopting the suggestions in this book, as well as about any condition that may require diagnosis or medical attention. The author and publisher disclaim any liability arising directly or indirectly from the use of this book.

POCKET BOOKS, a division of Simon & Schuster Inc.
1230 Avenue of the Americas, New York, NY 10020

Copyright © 1996 by Robert C. Fulford, D.O.
Introduction copyright © 1996 by Andrew Weil, M.D.

ISBN: 0-671-55600-2

First Pocket Books hardcover printing October 1996

10 9 8 7 6 5 4 3 2 1

POCKET and colophon are registered trademarks
of Simon & Schuster Inc.

Printed in the U.S.A

For my wife, Glenna

INTRODUCTION

In my recent book, *Spontaneous Healing*, I devoted a chapter to Dr. Robert Fulford, one of my teachers, the first who made me truly aware of the prodigious healing power of nature, which is now the focus of my work. I met Bob Fulford in Tucson, Arizona, in the early 1970s, when he was in his late sixties, supposedly in retirement but actually running a busy osteopathic practice from a small office on Grant Road. I spent many hours in that office watching the old doctor fix people by putting his hands on them and manipulating their bodies to allow the natural healing power to do its work. I marveled at the simplicity and effectiveness of his treatments, a striking contrast to the expensive, invasive high-tech medicine that had become the norm for most doctors—M.D.'s and D.O.'s alike.

In the years since then, conventional medicine has grown ever more expensive and complicated and as a result has gotten itself into deep economic trouble. As I write, the system is collapsing from its own weight, with hospitals going bankrupt, medical schools talking about mergers or closures, and doctors bemoaning the deadening influence of managed care on their lives. At the same time, consumers of health care are more and more dissatisfied with the services they are receiving, and in their dissatisfaction they are going to alternative providers in increasing numbers.

Osteopathic medicine, founded in 1874 by Andrew Taylor Still, was once a viable alternative to standard (or allopathic) medicine. Today it is practically indistinguishable from its onetime rival. Most contemporary D.O.'s give drugs and recommend surgery just like their M.D. colleagues. Few of them use manipulation at all, and fewer still rely on it as a main modality of treatment. Bob Fulford is therefore unusual in his own profession as well as in the world of modern medicine as a whole. His message about health and healing could not be more timely and important for doctors and patients alike.

In *Spontaneous Healing* I describe Bob Fulford as a man of strong hands and few words. He did not volunteer explanations of his methods and kept his philosophy to himself. When he did talk about medical problems and their treatment, he used language that was simple, never technical. I was surprised as well as pleased to learn that he had consented to help produce a book about his life and work.

In this book readers will not only learn the personal history of a remarkable healer, they will also discover many practical secrets of health and vitality, from the importance of proper breathing to the value of simple stretching as a superior tonic for nerves and muscles. Now in his nineties, Bob Fulford embodies and exemplifies his own wisdom about health and healing. He has led a remarkably vigorous life and had a remarkably productive old age, with little need for medical interventions.

As a physician dedicated to radical reform of medicine, I find Dr. Fulford's life and work a great inspiration for my work. His emphasis on vital energy and the healing power of nature—concepts that animated medical inquiry from the time of Hippocrates through the last century—is completely missing from medical education today. I once helped make a documentary video about this man, titled "Robert Fulford—An Osteopathic Alternative," but the more I think about it, the more I feel that his views are the mainstream of the evolution of medical thought and that it is twentieth-century technological medicine that has taken an alternative path, one that has led to an economic dead end. If medicine is to come back into alignment with the great healing traditions and satisfy the needs and desires of those who are sick, it must rediscover the truths that Bob Fulford expresses in these pages.

ANDREW WEIL, MD
Tucson, Arizona
January 1996

CONTENTS

PROLOGUE

Not too long ago I received a telephone call from a forty-five-year-old man in desperate need of help. For several months he had been suffering the symptoms of a heart attack, but he wasn't getting any relief from his doctors. The problem was that all the medical tests and electrocardiograms they had put him through didn't show anything wrong with the man's heart. Most physicians depend entirely upon tests and machines for their answers, and so, when the results showed that the heart appeared to be functioning normally, the doctors were mystified.

When the man asked whether someone should check out the rest of his body for the source of his problem, he was told no. If there was a problem in

1

the heart, the solution had to be in the heart, and that was the end of it.

As is often the case with those who become my patients, when no one else could uncover any answers, the man was referred to me.

Upon examining him I discovered that he had fractured his left thigh many years previously. After the surgeons repaired his leg, a good deal of fibrous tissue formed, and that in turn helped disturb certain muscles that lead up to the neck. These neck muscles may have contracted or become very loose and pliable, and therefore couldn't support the surrounding bones properly. One way or another, the man's balance was thrown off, and that distorted the cervical spinal column near the base of the skull, which is the source of the nerve supply to the heart. So the heart wasn't functioning correctly, not because it was ill, but because of an accident to the leg many years earlier.

It took four sessions of hands-on osteopathic manipulation (see page 14) for this man to regain his excellent health. Yet months later his doctors were still urging him to take more tests. They refused to believe that there was nothing wrong with his heart. They also refused to believe that anything other than their own familiar kind of medicine could help him.

Here's another story, about a young boy I met only a few months ago.

The boy's mother had endured terrible physical

difficulties during her pregnancy, and the child barely took in any air when he was born—which, as you will soon learn, is tantamount to a health crisis right from the start.

Soon after delivery the boy became ill, and for the next few years he was constantly coming down with pneumonia and other diseases. When he wasn't sick, he was a wild child, running around the house, bumping into walls, grabbing vases and ashtrays from tables and hurling them to the floor. On top of all that, he could barely talk, and his parents feared he was suffering from a mental disability.

Neither their pediatrician nor a child psychologist could offer the boy any help, and the parents were desperate.

Just after the boy's fourth birthday he was brought to see me. The moment I opened the front door of my home in rural Ohio, where I still practice, the boy ran right through it without saying a word, dashed over to the telephone and started yanking at the cord, trying to pull it to the floor.

It wasn't easy to get that boy to lie quietly on my table, but he finally settled down, and we had a good session. My first chore was to use my hands to loosen up his tailbone, and by doing so I was able to free up the recto-respiratory reflex, which stretches from the pelvis to the upper rib cage, where the lymphatic drainage from the ears takes place; if that reflex isn't in sync with the rest of the body, the lymphatic flow stagnates.

Although the boy was one of my most difficult cases, he's showing significant signs of improvement. He is beginning to breathe well, and as he does, he's calming down. His parents are quite grateful for both results. But what is most interesting is that the boy's speech level has risen close to that of his peer group. Whatever fears his parents had about any possible mental affliction have dissipated.

One of the lessons I have gleaned from my work is that physical and mental systems are connected. When patients leave my home after a successful treatment, not only do their bodies feel better, but often their minds have benefitted, too. The body and the mind are surely one, and help for one typically provides relief for the other.

One other recent case that I'll discuss in more depth later: this is the story of a doctor and his wife who had been looking forward to their fiftieth anniversary for many years. The plans they had made!—to travel, to relax, to enjoy their lives after many years of struggling to survive. But just before they were ready to leave, the wife developed symptoms of Alzheimer's disease, and the doctor, although experienced and capable, could only watch as she slipped into a vegetative state. Finally he was forced to place her in a nursing home.

The entire affair left the doctor deeply upset, both mentally and physically, as he had been taking constant care of his wife. He was completely enervated by the time she moved to the home, his mind listless, his spirit enfeebled.

It didn't take long for Mother Nature to finish the job. The doctor soon developed congestive heart failure, and would have died, slumped over his living-room chair, if his son hadn't happened to visit him just in time to rush him to the hospital.

Today the man is recovering well, and his own doctors say he could live many more years. But I know that what nearly killed the man wasn't a fragile heart, but the depression he felt over his wife's health, which weakened his spirit, causing his mind and body to suffer until they become vulnerable to attack. He recovered only when he made a decision to face up to the problem that caused his heart failure: he had started feeling responsible for his wife's condition. Of course that had made him unhappy. But once he realized that he had done as much as he could for her and that she would want him to be as healthy as possible, he was finally able to repair his spirit and his heart.

The human body is more complicated than an anatomy lesson might lead you to believe. Besides the systems and processes well known to everyone, the body is also composed of a complex interflowing stream of moving energy. When these energy streams become blocked or constricted, we lose the physical, emotional, and mental fluidity potentially available to us. If the blockage lasts long enough or is great enough, the result is pain, discomfort, illness, and distress.

My goal as a doctor is to help my patients open these energy blockages, for once the energy is unrestricted, the body can begin its own healing process. For instance, the hyperactive four-year-old boy responded well to my treatment, but it was his own internal powers of healing that, once activated, allowed his body to normalize itself.

This unblocking of energy can help the body, the mind, and even the spirit.

Unfortunately, most doctors don't believe this. As a result, contemporary medicine is facing a crisis. It insists on considering a human being merely as an object of science, which is a one-sided approach to treating symptoms. Symptoms must surely be understood, not merely combated.

The medical profession is based on scientific research, and while scientific research per se is valuable, there's more to healing than obtaining the test results of modern studies. For there are aspects to humanity that science will never explain, and these include morality, love, the spirit and the soul.

It is the task of our age to recognize humankind as a whole once more—each of us a being of spirit, mind, and body—without abandoning the knowledge we've gained through science. By studying the interrelationship of those three elements in detail, it will be possible for us to recognize that individual matter is the physical carrier for psychic or spiritual substances.

When we accomplish this, patients will no longer be regarded as if they were disease processes to be halted or problems to be solved, but as people in need of assistance in balancing their physical, mental, and spiritual dimensions. Without question this should be the new direction of modern medicine, and it is one that is long overdue.

1

The Elements of Osteopathy

For the last half a century I have worked as an osteopath. It's a career that has afforded me great fulfillment, and I have treated thousands of patients with a very high degree of success. Yet I am constantly surprised by osteopathy's low profile. Few people know what it's all about, nor are they aware of the marvelous things that it can accomplish.

Osteopathy and osteopathic manipulation were developed by Dr. Andrew Taylor Still (1828–1917), a fourth-generation American of Scottish ancestry. He was an early supporter of women's suffrage and an opponent of slavery who fought for the North in the Civil War, serving as both a soldier and surgeon. But, returning to his conventional medical practice when the war ended, Dr. Still became dissatisfied with the state of contemporary medicine, which at the time basically consisted of three schools: homeopathy, allopathy, and eclectic medicine.

Homeopathy, established by Dr. Samuel Hahnemann (1755–1843), is based on the idea that diseases can be cured by prescribing microscopic doses of medications that produce in patients the same symptoms as the disease itself.

Allopathy remains the most common form of medicine practiced today. During Dr. Still's time, allopaths were noted for their primary reliance on drugs to cure diseases.

The eclectic school, as its name implies, borrowed from many others and was loosely monitored and often erratically practiced.

Dr. Still was unhappy with all of these approaches and, in particular, he disliked the nineteenth century's fascination with drugs. Instead, he investigated the possibility of a medical procedure that would rely on the body's own natural healing properties.

Dr. Still observed that whenever he found disease in a patient, he also found problems in the body's musculoskeletal system, and he suspected that imbalances in the circulation and nervous systems were causing these problems. His solution was to manipulate the body with the hands so as to restore proper circulation. Dr. Still was convinced he had found a valuable tool for helping humankind. He named it osteopathy, from the Greek root words, *osteo*, meaning bone, and *pathos*, to suffer.

When few people accepted his theories, Dr. Still became his own missionary, traveling across America throughout the 1870s and 1880s to demonstrate his new techniques. Eventually he was able to interest enough advocates to found, in Kirksville, Missouri, the American School of Osteopathy. The college granted the degree of Doctor of Osteopathy (DO), instead of the allopathic Doctor of Medicine (MD). That was in 1892. From then on, mostly by word of mouth, osteopathy flourished.

During the first two decades of the twentieth century, medical education, which had been basically unsupervised in the United States, began receiving careful scrutiny. And as the allopathic practitioners had grown to become the most politically powerful discipline and were united in the powerful American Medical Association (AMA), their schools soon eclipsed all others. In particular, the AMA fought against its foremost rival, osteopathy, which the allopathic physicians called quackish and almost succeeded in suppressing entirely. Among other tactics, the AMA announced that if osteopaths were allowed to practice in the armed forces during World War I, allopathic doctors would refuse to do so. A similar strategy was also used during World War II, although ironically this stance proved beneficial to osteopaths, because those who stayed behind found their practices prospering. Many Americans who otherwise might not have been introduced to osteopathy tried it in the absence of M.D.'s and were successfully treated. Still, osteopathy struggled against numerous state laws that either restricted or forbade its use.

The second half of the century has been kinder to osteopathy. Despite continuing opposition from the AMA, states slowly began to license osteopaths; now all fifty have come into accord, while at the same time many more osteopathic colleges have been founded and brought under the jurisdiction of state boards. In 1969–70 Michigan established the first state-supported osteopathic college; in 1972 the Oklahoma legislature created the College of Osteopathic Medicine and Surgery, and soon afterward several other schools were instituted, again under the aegis of state governments.

There are currently thirty thousand osteopaths in America, which is more than double the number twenty-five years ago. Students can attend one of fifteen osteopathic schools, studying a curriculum similar to that of their allopathic counterparts, except that in addition most students learn manipulation. Today the allopathic and osteopathic forces have made their peace with each other, and in many hospitals you'll find the two types of doctors with different degrees working side by side. In fact, I have found that nearly all of my referrals have come from MDs rather than from other DOs.

* * *

Today too many medical doctors believe that the body is composed of thousands of unrelated systems. They operate on the construction-work model—as when an electric wire is in the wrong position relative to the new rafter and has to be moved, but the carpenter refuses to do the rewiring; he's got to call an electrician. In allopathic medicine, if your internist decides your heart is ailing, off you go to a cardiologist. If the problem lies in your stomach, you visit a gastroenterologist. But these doctors aren't looking at the whole body, and therefore they often miss the real source of the problem.

Osteopaths prefer a holistic approach. We believe each human body is composed of many "bodies," such as the body of blood vessels, the body of the nervous system, the body of muscles, the body of the bony structure, and so on. All these bodies are fundamentally connected to one another, and you can't have good health in one without having it in all the others. At the heart of osteopathy, then, is the belief that well-being depends on the maintenance of proper relationships among the various body systems. That was why I was able to help the man who came to see me for a bad heart: it wasn't his heart that was causing his problem.

And "helped" is a key word. An osteopath believes that a body has the ability to heal itself. We don't do all the work ourselves. Once we're through, the body takes over.

* * *

Although osteopaths and medical doctors rely on many similar procedures, including drugs, X-rays, and surgery, osteopaths also treat the human body with our hands in a process Dr. Still called manipulation. The part of the body we manipulate is what I call the bony structure (although these days many people call this the musculoskeletal system) which consists of the bones, muscles, tendons, joints, and tissues.

This system forms the support structure for the rest of the body. When you build a house, the rafters have to be finished and stable before the siding can be applied. Likewise, without a well-tuned, sturdy bony structure, you can't have good health, for defects in this structure influence the body's natural functions.

How does the body respond to osteopathic manipulation? Manipulation stimulates the flow of the body's cerebrospinal fluid, which bathes the surfaces of the brain and the spinal cord. It also increases the body's respiration, helping to put more oxygen into the bloodstream, which also aids in digestion, delivering energy to the body more efficiently. Thus manipulation restores the balance in the digestion, respiration, circulation and brain functions.

Perhaps the primary reason I became an osteopath was to show allopathic doctors that they had made a mistake by not admitting me to their medical school.

The faculty at the University of Louisville, across the river from where I grew up in Ohio, had promised to accept me if I repeated a course in organic chemistry. And so I did. But on the last day of class my professor told me to see the dean of the Medical School. I went to his office, where he asked me to sit down, hee-hawed around a little bit, and finally said that he felt I would make a much better dentist than a doctor. I never found out how he came to that conclusion, but I knew that it meant I was no longer accepted to the school.

The rejection stung, but a few years later a friend who had attended the Kansas City School of Osteopathic Medicine told me about Dr. Still's discipline and its philosophy. I made a quick decision, packed up my bags, and showed up in Kansas City two weeks after classes had begun. The staff glanced at my record and all they said was that I wouldn't have to repeat organic chemistry.

At that time, the Kansas City college placed a heavy emphasis on developing the sensitive touch students needed to become skillful manipulators. To help us, our professors would take human bones, wrap them up inside blankets, and hand us the package. We were expected to describe what we felt without looking inside. By doing so, we were developing the ability to detect with our hands what osteopaths call blockages, or distortions, in the body.

This kind of training composed a significant portion of our study. When I was in school, medical doctors took 3,800 hours of training and osteopaths 4,200; the additional hours were devoted to the manipulation classes.

For practice, my classmates and I would often work on one another's bodies. I was in pretty good condition, but we quickly learned to be careful when applying such a powerful technique. One day a classmate tried a certain kind of manipulation on my left shoulder and caused me to come down with a terrible flu. It turned out that he had mistakenly blocked out the lymphatic areas in my left lung.

In another test at school, we would take one human hair and place it on a piece of plain paper, and then put another sheet of paper over that. There could be no writing or lines on the paper to guide us. Next we took each finger and went over the paper until we could feel the little ridge of the hair beneath. And when we could do this with all ten fingers, our professors would add another sheet on top of the last, and we tried again, and again, until we were unable to go further.

My reputation as someone who could feel the slightest ripple through paper grew to the point that one day, when I was giving a lecture at a Tucson, Arizona, hospital, a doctor in the audience pulled a hair out of the head of the woman sitting next to him—I could see her jerk when he did it—and then came up to the podium. He placed the hair under eighteen pieces of paper and challenged me in front of the audience to find it. Well, of course I was able to do it, but for the life of me I couldn't figure out why he didn't just pluck a hair from his own head.

I have never stopped trying to develop the sense of touch. Today my hands are sensitive enough to tell you where you might have broken a bone many dozens of years past. I just move my hand down the limb until I feel a little rough edge, a drag in the muscles, and the added calcium that formed on the bone when it healed.

After graduating from Kansas City, I came to Ohio to practice. Over the years I've seen thousands of patients, ranging in age from three days to eighty-five years. Now, as I start my tenth decade, I prefer working only with the young. That's not because I like them better, although I do enjoy a child's glow. More important than that, I just don't have enough physical stamina to work on adults day after day. Adults emit less energy than children; they give back little while you give them everything, which causes me to feel depleted. Children, who are more radiant, don't absorb my energy in the same way.

When I first started my practice, I wasn't able to perform manipulation as much as I wanted, for most allopathic doctors were serving overseas in World War II and I had to work eighteen to twenty hours a day, doing everything possible to help whoever needed me. Back then we didn't have enough doctors in the hospitals to meet patient demand, so every time patients called us, we had to attend to them, at whatever hour of the day.

After the war, when the other doctors returned, I set myself up as an osteopath in Cincinnati. For the first three months no one showed up. I just sat, waited, and read dozens of books. Then a neighborhood priest visiting the barbershop across the street asked the barber what he knew about me. The barber replied that he knew nothing at all.

So the priest came over and introduced himself. We soon became friends and spent quite a few evenings together at nightclubs across the river in Kentucky. This priest seemed to open the door for my practice, because, thanks to his referrals, I never had any more time to myself. Eventually I attracted too many patients and had to turn them over to an intern who shared my office space.

Without doubt, the highlight of my career has been my patients' kind response. Every week I receive cards and letters from people who seem grateful for my work. Nothing could make me feel better than the knowledge that those people for whom I cared have appreciated that effort.

During the years of osteopathy's political drive for official recognition, the profession started emulating allopathic medicine. The reasoning may have been that if osteopaths became more like medical doctors, the profession's chances for acceptance would improve. And perhaps this strategy has been successful.

But I think my peers took the wrong path, because osteopaths began to devalue their manipulation training, and students were not required to be as well versed in it as they had been when I was in school.

Today that's changing. Osteopathy is well established, and many students pursue it because they want to use their hands to work with the body in this rewarding way. What is most gratifying to me is that so many young doctors want to return to the profession's roots and use their hands rather than drugs to cure their patients.

You must keep in mind that not all osteopaths think as I do. I find it heartening, however, that today it's the young ones who are most likely to agree with me.

I believe that osteopathy has a bright future. This is because the universe is run by specific laws that, taken together, constitute a philosophy. Osteopathy, too, has a philosophy that reflects these universal laws. Working as an osteopath involves applying these laws to human beings, which enables the osteopath to delve into the deepest causes of a medical problem. This book will attempt to explain some of this philosophy.

Besides a philosophy, osteopathy is also an art. Art is the skill or power to perform certain actions. And osteopathy is a science. Science is a systematized knowledge of nature and the physical.

The osteopathic profession has grown as a seed does. First it established its roots in the soil—society. Then it cracked the soil open—attained governmental recognition. The stem of the seed has since broken through the soil. Now it is osteopathy's time to mature and bloom. Because its philosophy, art, and science are based on health promotion, disease prevention, and a natural approach to patients, I am confident that osteopathy will come into its full flower in the twenty-first century.

2

A Brief Account of the Universe

The material universe is bound together as though it were one, and its various parts are as interdependent as our own vital functions, none of which can be affected without influencing the whole body. Therefore, humans aren't citizens merely of this world, but of the universe in all its parts, visible and invisible.

In order to understand our health, we must own a basic understanding of the world around us. Few people consider how much nature and their bodies actually interact. Yet most of us are aware of studies showing that the moon's waxing and waning plays a principal role in the twenty-eight-day female menstrual cycle. The rising and falling barometer affect us, too. Even as I'm writing this, a storm is blowing across the plains into Ohio, and as it does, my respiration is becoming difficult and my mind is growing weary. A falling barometer upsets my inner chemistry and tightens my system.

What good can come from knowing our relationship to the universe? Once we understand how nature functions, we appreciate it more, and a higher appreciation of nature leads to a better comprehension of our place in it, which in turn can only lead to a fuller understanding of our health.

A businessperson might respond, that's all very well and good, but I just want to make money. To that I would answer, are you going to take that money with you, or are you going to leave it behind? What I'm talking about is something you're going to take with you.

THE LIFE FIELD

It is my firm belief, after more than a half century of reading, debating, questioning, and contemplating, that the human body is surrounded by something that I call a life field.

This life field thoroughly permeates the physical body and actually reaches beyond it by many inches. To imagine what it might look like, you might want to think of a colored aura surrounding the body, one that might appear green or red or yellow, or any other color, depending on the individual. I've been told that my own life field has a bluish tint, which indicates that I'm more of a healing than a spiritual person, who would have a purple-tinged aura.

If you could see the field, it would resemble a human shadow: the field's pattern surrounds the head, spreading out around the shoulders and becoming narrower by the waist, and then tapering down the legs to the feet. In some ways, the life field could be considered the body's other half: the spatial part is the portion we commonly think of as the material human being, while the other half is this invisible field.

At one time researchers could only detect the field to a quarter of an inch away from the body, but recent experiments have found it extending as far away as thirty inches.

This life field conveys vitality to your physical body and provides you with your spirit. Whenever you feel a disturbance or an injury, the life field manifests its shock in the physical body with a depletion of energy. If left unchecked, this deficiency can lead to dysfunction, disease, and, ultimately, to the body's total collapse; but if the deficiency is discovered and restored, the body can repair the health that it has lost.

The clearest sign of an unsound life field is the state of your health: the worse it is, the worse your field.

I first learned about this life field from the work of Dr. Harold Saxon Burr, formerly a professor of neuroanatomy at the Yale University School of

Medicine, who discovered that the human body is imbued in, and surrounded by, energy in the form of electricity.

In 1935 Dr. Burr conceived an experiment in which he attached voltmeters to a peach tree outside his kitchen, allowing him to record the electromagnetic activity taking place in and around the tree. He also hooked up two other trees, which were about forty-five miles removed from each other, and studied them for many years.

From his research, Dr. Burr discovered that each tree was surrounded by an electromagnetic field, and that this field was clearly responding to the tree's life, changing in voltage whenever the tree bloomed or its leaves fell, and reacting to major weather conditions, such as the sun's shifting spots, the moon's waxing and waning, as well as to rain, snow, sleet, and hailstorms. All these elements affected the voltage potential of the trees, sometimes lowering it, sometimes raising it.

Dr. Burr also found that, as one of the trees began to wither, its voltage steadily dropped and continued to do so until it reached zero. At that moment the tree died.

Other plants responded to these various cosmic forces with changes in their voltage patterns, which convinced Dr. Burr that the human body must also react to those same forces and led him to experiments that verified his theories. Among his subsequent findings were that a woman's voltage rises dramatically in the course of ovulation.

Dr. Burr also discovered that human voltage changes during the cycle of a disease process, and that some of these shifts can occur a considerable amount of time before the disease itself can be clinically detected.

Based on his findings, Dr. Burr declared: "Wherever there is life, there are electrical properties."

The life field, therefore, is an electric field with a high frequency. Dr. Burr always spoke of it as the "organizing field" for the physical body, claiming that the life field actually appeared before the physical body itself, in order to guide the atoms and molecules of a growing organism into its proper form.

In a sense, the electromagnetic pattern creates a mold, which is eventually filled by matter, giving rise to a tangible, material body. Both the material body and the field have their own "brains," but the life-field brain is nothing like the physical brain; it's more of an organizing pattern that maintains the structure of an organism and also instructs the body's new cells—the ones that replace those cells constantly dying within us— where they belong in the human body. How else would cells know to travel into the liver or into the muscles or into the lungs?

Reading about Dr. Burr's work on the life field caused me to question some of the knowledge I had acquired in school. Then, in the early 1940s, it was my privilege to attend a lecture on this life field given by Dr. Leonard Ravitz, one of Dr. Burr's assistants. Dr. Ravitz had been kind enough to bring with him from Yale the instruments that Dr. Burr had used to determine the life field. This allowed me a chance to experience the work firsthand.

Dr. Ravitz invited four of us at a time to visit his hotel room, where he had set up his equipment. He hooked the instruments to one of our index fingers and then placed them in a salt solution, showing us on the meters how the current changed—and how each of us had a different voltage.

One of the measurements Dr. Burr and Dr. Ravitz had compared during their studies, and which Dr. Ravitz now revealed to us, was the difference in voltage in the right and left hands. If an individual is well-balanced, the voltage in the two hands will register equally on each side, like an alternating current. This turned out to be the case for all four of us in the hotel room those five decades ago. If the voltage of the sides had varied, however, it could have disclosed an impending disease process—just as when you put two electric wires together and they spark rather than turning on a light, indicating a problem within the wire's circuitry.

I was dumbfounded by these demonstrations. My schooling had convinced me that all answers existed in the standard anatomy, physiology, and pathology texts. I had no place for such new ideas.

But when something so curious arises, although the temptation is to disbelieve, because that is so much easier, a better alternative is to open the mind to the possibility that your assumptions have legitimately been challenged. And when further examination only serves to prove the new information's accuracy, it's time to embrace it, even if this means changing your worldview. Something inside me said that this research pointed to the proper path for my life's work, and I have found it a very successful road indeed.

Outside the West, this concept of vital energy has been accepted for thousands of years. The Chinese call it *chi*, the Japanese call it *ki*, and the Hindus *prana*. Unfortunately, in America we don't really have a name for it.

For many years few people gave Dr. Burr's experimentation much credence, because it stood so far apart from conventional scientific wisdom. In fact, if Dr. Burr hadn't been the editor of the *Yale Journal of Biology and Medicine*, he probably wouldn't have been able to find any forum whatsoever, as it is unlikely that another medical journal would have published his work. But over the last decade much new research has been undertaken on the subject, and the field even has a name now: energy medicine.

Many others have investigated this life field, including Dr. Valerie V. Hunt while she was at the University of California at Los Angeles in the 1980s. Her findings have indicated that the whole body may indeed be an electromagnetic field. Dr. Hunt worked with a dancer in a special room equipped so that its magnetic field could be decreased and its electrical field lowered, and vice versa. Whenever the magnetic field was removed, the dancer developed hectic, scattered, and incoherent movements. The action of the remaining environmental electrical field caused the dancer to experience a neurological disturbance and disorientation in space. When the magnetic field was increased, however, the dancer's body movements became more coordinated.

Today, the usefulness of electricity as a diagnostic aide is universally recognized; the widespread use of such common tools as the electrocardiogram and the electroencephalogram are testimony to some of Dr. Burr's ideas. But medicine has yet to tap the full potential of Dr. Burr's work in predicting and diagnosing other conditions.

There are those who believe that many of the phenomena in living organisms can be accounted for by ordinary physical and chemical forces. The biologist maintains that whatever remains, whatever is unexplained, can be known once we learn more about biological actions. The chemist, interested only in the chemical processes, believes once we have advanced our chemical education, we will understand. The physicist is anticipating further discoveries in the subatomic. Life for these people is an interesting playground of molecular structures. But there's more to life than mechanics, because these types of explanations are never complete. They're lacking that one critical element: the life field, the creative force of the universe.

For instance, I have a chair in front of me, and I can try to analyze the elements of what produced that chair. The makers rounded wood to construct the legs, and other wood was contoured so that I can sit on it comfortably. The chair was finally pinned together so that it won't collapse when it receives my weight. In the end, though, we have little knowledge of how the wood that constitutes the chair came into being in the first place. Scientists don't have that answer today, and perhaps they never will.

THE LIFE FORCE

The life field, which envelops and surrounds the body, is composed of electromagnetic energy. This energy also exists within the body, in a form I call the life force.

My notion of the life force doesn't arise from complex metaphysical or philosophical doctrines. It's based on simple observation and a workaday understanding completely accessible to anyone, and it's something that all my years of experience with patients tells me is true.

The eminent psychoanalyst Wilhelm Reich once described the sensation of the life force as a prickling feeling. After much research, Reich came to believe that this energy existed not only within the human organism, but externally as well, in the form of cosmic forces.

Others besides Dr. Burr and Reich have written about the life force, but certainly one reason I believe in its existence is that I have grown to depend on it for my practice. Without my knowledge of the life force, I simply couldn't have helped people. Due in part to my osteopathic manipulative training, my hands have become sensitive enough over the years to perceive when this energy is moving well through the body and when it's blocked.

Many people have asked me what the life force feels like beneath my fingers. There are no words to convey this sensation but the best I can do is to ask if you have ever felt your body tingle. That's close to what I feel, just as Reich described. When I run my hands over a patient with a healthy, vibrant life force, I pick up that same prickling in my hands. If, however, my fingers stick rather than glide, here the body is static and the life force is being blocked.

Sometimes I've had patients in whom I can barely feel any of the life force. I refer to these people as blanks, because that's what they feel like to me: the life force isn't flowing, and so, when I run my hand over their bodies, I feel a drag, and my hand won't slide past a certain spot. Much of the life force's flow is regulated by the mind. As I will explain later, the mind controls the body, and thus the individual's emotional reactions can tighten up or block his or her physical being. Such people are letting their instincts rather than their reason govern them.

At other times I touch patients whose bodies are brimming with so much life force that I feel exhilarated around them. Sadly, however, this is rare.

Anyone with sufficiently sensitive hands can feel this magnetic field. For others who wish to develop this sense, I recommend the way I learned, which is how I still train young doctors: place a hair beneath a piece of paper and slowly run the fingers over it until the hair can be felt. This method will stimulate all the nerve fibers in the finger. It even worked for one student whose hands were once as rough as a coal miner's; he now has a very successful pediatric practice in Tucson.

The following is an example of how I interact with my patients' life force. I recently saw a man in his early fifties who was in terrible physical condition—listless, incapable of working, ready to die. He had already consulted with several medical doctors, but despite repeated tests, no one could locate the source of his difficulty. For lack of a solution, they sent him to a hospital; there they decided the problem might lie in his gallbladder, and so they removed it.

But the gallbladder wasn't the answer. The man's health continued to decline, and because the doctors had no more answers, they sent him back home. Not long afterward the man called me and asked, in a very weak voice, if I would see him. Although at this point in my practice I don't normally work with adults, he'd been through so much I felt obliged to examine him.

When I did, I asked him to tell me about any accidents in his past, because my examination of his body had revealed some trauma in his rib area. He replied, somewhat surprised, that seventeen years previously he had been driving up a road on a steep hill when he hit a car coming up the other side.

I knew immediately that the shock of that accident was still in his system and it had closed down his life force for all that time, causing the man to deteriorate slowly.

I manipulated him for about ten minutes. Right afterward he said he could feel vigorous energy rattling through his body. In a few more minutes he could raise himself off the table. Within another half an hour he was standing up, thoroughly enjoying this movement of the life force.

As in any other accident, an automobile collision causes you to hold your breath, which in effect means that you're blocking the flow of energy through your body, and for many, that flow never fully returns.

Recently another patient came to see me after he developed symptoms that his doctors diagnosed as vagotonia, which creates a feeling similar to that of having a heart attack. He would be sitting in a chair watching television, and then, without warning, he'd feel a terrible pain in his chest. His doctor would whisk him off to the emergency room, but no one could ever diagnose a problem.

When he lay down on my table, I started examining him, and I could immediately feel, just from touching his ankle, that there was little life in the left side of his body. I asked my favorite question: did you ever get into an accident as a child? The man responded that he had; his left leg had been broken and the doctors had performed surgery on it.

There's your problem, I said. We then went to work to break up the fibrotic tissue that had formed where the surgery had taken place, and we also leveled out his pelvis by placing a little lift in his left heel. It turned out that the scar tissue in the muscle was blocking the life force through his left side; it had created a little shortness there from a slight spinal curvature that happened to press against the heart's nerve supply.

The man took a deep, long breath when we were finished. I sent him home with some exercises to reinforce his breathing, and to this day he hasn't suffered a single recurrence.

Since the dawn of history, every civilization has sought to define life's spiritual side. These efforts have led to diverse results, from a pantheon of anthropomorphic gods to the worship of primeval nature or of a single, great deity. To my mind, what is spiritual in the world is the universal source of this cosmic electrical energy, this life force that keeps us all alive.

I suspect that this universal life force may well be another name for God, or the universal creator. And I believe that God, therefore, exists within all of us, embodied in this energy. Most people today have been schooled to believe that God exists without, rather than within themselves. I think this is a mistake.

Certainly, if you believe that God is within, you will start to take much better care of your body, for your body truly is your temple.

VIBRATIONS

Nothing rests. Everything vibrates. Everything, in some subtle way, moves.

What brings the corn shoot out of the earth when you've covered up the seed? How does a chick get out of its shell? Everything is vibratory.

Every living thing pulses with the flow of the electric life force that pervades the universe. This vibration can't be seen, but it can be felt, with your hands, with your fingers. I have developed to a point where I can feel this vibration when I place my hands on certain trees, on dogs and cats, and of course, on the human body.

Most people understand the concept of the vibrations of the color spectrum, in which each color is differentiated by its frequency; every high school student who's taken basic science knows about the colors of the rainbow and why red and violet are on opposite ends of the spectrum. Vibrations also produce sound, whether music or words. In fact, every human response is a vibratory one.

We respond to most vibrations, or, as I prefer, we appreciate the work of Mother Nature, through our senses—sight, taste, smell, hearing, and touch. But each of us responds to these vibrations individually, because we vary in our sensitivity to them. Your appreciation of a beautiful panoramic view may be altogether different from mine. Perhaps you're a little more sensitive than I am and can pick up a higher vibration, causing you to see coloration more vividly than I do. The color red to you may look different from how it looks to me, just as two persons may hear the same musical note differently.

This is true even in conversation. We don't always hear the same words similarly, not because of interpretation, but because of vibration. Likewise, we taste through vibration, and the way you taste sweetness, for instance, isn't necessarily equivalent to the way I do.

These vibrations can lead to trouble as well as pleasure when our desires come into the picture. A beautiful song enters your mind through sound waves, and you like it so much you decide you must possess it. Hearing those vibrations stimulates a desire within the mind, and sometimes that kind of desire can be quite unhealthy. A recording of a song is easy to buy, but what if it's a chocolate cake that attracts you, or a bar of gold? These may emanate alluring vibrations, but it might not always be wise to pursue them.

Vibrations affect human health, too. When I've been working on patients who, through manipulation, are opened up, their bodies begin to tingle. This means that the patient's life field has synchronized with the material body, and they feel that vibration.

Everyone is always vibrating, but when a part of the body isn't vibrating well, the life force isn't flowing smoothly. Those are the times when I sense a drag in the body's tissues as I move my hand over it.

I recently saw a young woman whose goal is to become a professional golfer. She's extremely talented, but one day she hurt her wrist while swinging her club, and the pain wouldn't abate. When no other doctor was able to help her, she came to me.

The moment I began my examination I could feel the drag all the way from her shoulder down to her hand; there was no vibration, meaning something was wrong with the muscle tissue. So I sat her down and did a little manipulation, opening up her life force, bringing her wrist back to normalcy, and before long she was able to return to her golf game.

All people vibrate at their own particular frequency. In the work done by Dr. Valerie Hunt, personal frequencies were seen as an indicator of a body's potential. Someone with a low frequency can have a career playing football or lifting heavy barrels. But someone whose frequency is in the mid-range will have a more delicate body, although their capacity to engage in mental work, to produce thought patterns, will be greater.

A very intuitive person will log in with a high frequency; the higher the frequency, the more spiritual the person.

I always tell my young patients that there's no point participating in athletics if your body isn't the sort that can handle the stress. I have never understood why such people still insist on playing rough sports.

When you are vibrating well, you are healthy. When your vibration rate is off, then you are suffering some sort of disease process. It's too bad that so few people can recognize their body's optimal vibratory rate. I've always thought that the best way to achieve this is to meditate, because it quiets the mind and puts one in touch with inner rhythms (see Chapter 5). But there aren't many willing to meditate regularly.

Of course, another way to test your vibration level is to see a good osteopath.

BREATH

Mankind is not fed by bread alone, but also by breath. The bread taken into the stomach feeds the muscles and blood, while the breath taken into the lungs feeds the nervous system.

A life is defined by breath: you take your first breath when you're born, and your last the moment you die.

One cycle of food lasts twenty-four hours, for it takes that long to enter and leave your body via digestion. One cycle of respiration, or digestion of air, takes about three seconds.

Breath is the means by which you are connected to the universe: without the breath, there would be no consciousness. The breath builds and repairs the structure of the physical body, and it maintains a balance between the building material and the waste matter that can't otherwise be removed.

You can gauge the essential nature of breath by the fact that you can live without food for a number of weeks, without drink for a few days, but without air, you can live only a few minutes. You can even temporarily relinquish consciousness, as in deep sleep or under narcosis, but you can't abandon breathing as long as you are alive.

Breathing is the only vital function that, in spite of its independence from your normal consciousness, is nevertheless accessible to your mind. In contrast, you have very little control over your digestive processes or over the beating of your heart, the circulation of your blood, the currents of your nerve energy, the functions of assimilation, secretion, etc.

Breathing is different. It will keep going when

you're not aware of it, and at the same time, if you want to take a deep breath you can consciously do so.

What this means is that you have the capacity to bring your conscious intelligence to your breathing, to take more of the life force into your body. Breathing represents your best opportunity to regulate and maximize the all-important flow of the vital life force in your body and your life. Opportunity *and* responsibility—you owe it to yourself to breathe well. I will tell you how.

Within every single breath you take there exist four divisions: the physical breath, the breath form, the life breath, and the light breath.

The majority of people, as they breathe, are moving their diaphragm and taking in air, but that's it. This *physical breath* is the one most people know best; it supports the physical body and gives you the opportunity to be active.

The second part of breath, the *breath form*, helps to maintain the structure of the body. It determines the body's pattern. If you take in breath poorly, your upper ribs, for instance, may be bent forward, and you may develop bad posture as a result. I've seen hundreds of children whose posture has improved dramatically after opening up their ribs through osteopathic manipulation.

The third type of breath is the *life breath*, which gives life to the body. It enters the body with that first breath you take as a baby and helps stoke the body with continuing life throughout existence.

You can see this breath in another person's eyes: it resembles a glow emanating from within. People who have a great deal of life in them almost radiate, and this comes from the life breath.

Finally there is the *light breath*, which is what I call the breath that feeds the soul. This energy is part of the spiritual force of the universal energy, and it enters your body with every breath.

Everyone takes in some breath, of course, but you must take in all four types in order for the entire body to function properly, and the only way to do that is through deep, full breathing. In other words, although you can't see these four breaths enter your body, they do so each time you inhale if your breathing is good and deep.

To see if you are taking in air well, hold a mirror under your nose and observe the moisture that forms on the mirror's surface when you exhale: if an equal amount appears from each nostril, you are most likely breathing well.

During the course of a day, the average person breathes approximately twenty-eight thousand times. If you observed closely, you would find that each of these breaths brings a new thought to mind or a new turn to an old thought. For if a breath is being taken in properly, the life breath will be stimulating the brain cells, which helps spark the mind.

Whenever your physical body has been stressed and you feel fatigue, by inhaling a deep breath through the nostrils, holding it for a number of seconds, and then suddenly expelling it, also through the nostrils, you can strip your unwanted feelings from the body and bring it into a state of balance and well-being.

Remember: always try to breathe through your nostrils, and not your mouth, because air must contact the olfactory nerves to stimulate your brain and put it into its natural rhythm. If you don't breathe through your nose, in a sense you're only half alive.

As a person breathes, so is that person.

Those times when a person breathes poorly indicate poor health and low energy. This is particularly true after a trauma, which jams the life force, keeping the breath from flowing properly through the body (see Chapter 4).

For many, birth is the first major trauma. The baby's body takes on a compact form for delivery, and after a gentle birth, as the baby swallows a healthy first breath of air, the body is reassembled, unfolded. Unfortunately, this process doesn't occur properly in many births, and the body never fully expands, making it predisposed to imbalance and distortion.

People also harm the breathing process through physical or psychological trauma, which produces a shock that causes most of us to hold our breath and lock it. I believe that this, perhaps more than any other factor, causes such shock to give rise to a traumatic effect; when the breath is jammed, your life energy is weakened at a moment when you need it most. That trauma leads to a continuing pattern of abnormal behavior that seeps into the body and remains there, creating negative effects.

Thus, the more the breath is freed, the less the effect of the trauma.

Poor breathing can also result in poor performance and even childhood learning disabilities. If the breath isn't deep and doesn't reach completely into the diaphragm, the toxins in the bloodstream aren't being transferred over to the outgoing breath, and this can cause a great deal of trouble in the brain, because its functioning depends upon its receiving a proper blood supply.

Learn to breathe deeply and well—try out the exercises in Chapter 8—and, above all, breathe in a loving way. As we all breathe together, we become one in thought and being.

THOUGHTS ARE THINGS

The life field is a web of energy streams, of lines of light and force, and it radiates color, depending on your spiritual evolvement.

Furthermore, the field changes every time you shift your thought patterns or are stirred emotionally.

For instance, if you become overly attached to a thought pattern imbued with a high emotional content, that thought pattern will become locked into the life field. This will cause a reaction in the physical body, such as a slumping of the shoulders, a shortening of the leg, or a pulling of the eye muscles. If continued for an extended period of time, these patterns will become chronic and lock into the body's form permanently.

One of the experiments carried on by Dr. Ravitz, Dr. Burr's assistant, involved hypnotizing patients and implanting in them a simple idea. Dr. Ravitz discovered that these implanted thoughts dramatically changed the life field's voltage. He also found that certain states of mind in people who were conscious, such as the formation of an unspoken thought or image, affect this voltage, too.

In other words, your thoughts have physical consequences, so you should be aware of what you are thinking and how you act upon those thoughts.

For example, not long ago a young mother came to my home with a five-year-old child suffering from an odd ailment that doctors couldn't remedy. Whenever the parents took the child outside for a walk, he would break away, run over to strangers, and bite them.

Before beginning my examination, I asked the mother if any physical or emotional trauma had taken place during her pregnancy. She said no. All the mother knew was that the child, for as long as he'd been walking, had been biting people. But after we had talked for some time, the mother revealed that two suicides had occurred in her extended family just before the child was born. It was clear to me that his biting resulted from the mother's emotional response to the suicides. The child hadn't liked his mother's thoughts, and anger and pain still resided inside him.

By manipulating the boy's bony structure, we removed the shock and loosened up his spinal column. When the treatment ended, the boy rose from the table, climbed onto his mother's lap and fell asleep. As far as I know, he's never bitten anyone again.

Few pregnant women are warned that their thoughts affect their child, as do the father's (see Chapter 6). It's perfectly natural for both mother and father to have all kinds of negative thoughts during a pregnancy—no one can stave off depressing, unhappy moments for nine months. But parents who have endured particularly severe psychic or emotional trauma during pregnancy should be aware that the resulting thoughts may well have taken root in the child, producing physical or psychological symptoms with no apparent relation to their origin, but which may require action. Parents of children with inexplicable, recurring symptoms may want to reflect on the period of the pregnancy to see if any sustained negative thoughts could be responsible for the current condition.

Besides an osteopathic examination, another of my recommendations to help children is the use of nursery rhymes and lullabies. By chanting the singsong cadences of verses like "Rock-a-Bye, Baby," a parent can help plant the rhythm of the life force back into the child.

Another form of thought, desire, can also bring on an illness.

Let's say you have a desire to accomplish something, and over time you nourish that desire, feeding and stoking it, until one day something happens to thwart your ambition. This upset can disturb your body's chemistry, and you could come down with an illness in a day or two, or feel so sick that you should go to bed, whether you want to or not. (Often people who should take care of their body after a setback don't. They think it's more important to work than rest, because their desire is to get paid and please the boss. Even when they do stay home, they can't relax and they do everything but lie still.)

Let's say a teenage boy wants a new car. Perhaps for a year the boy's hopes have been high, and during that time he's been anticipating what the car is going to look like, how he's going to enjoy driving it, and what his friends will think. But then his father says no, he can't buy the boy a car. Either the boy accepts his father's decision, which is rare, or he goes into a state of depression. Why won't his father let him have that car? he asks himself, repeating it over and over in his mind. By doing so he gradually upsets the balance of his nervous system.

These kinds of processes can last a lifetime. I frequently have patients who arrive complaining about aches and pains, but when I get them to open up, they begin relating the thought patterns that began in childhood, making it clear how closely associated their illness is with old patterns they never broke, the issues they never dealt with. Once this happens, there's a good chance their health will improve.

I wish I could say I have encountered many examples of this process working the other way, where people were able to correct their body chemistry with positive thoughts. I haven't. But I comfort myself with the thought that these people do exist, but they simply have no reason to consult with me, for they know how to take care of themselves.

Whenever you think, energy is emitted from your body. Observe people who try to get their points across with their hands: they are projecting their life field to influence your own. This is basically what any good salesperson does. And since the majority of their customers don't have the sensitivity to feel the field consciously, such salespeople are often writing up their orders before anyone knows what happened.

It's necessary to keep the mind in a state of balance and creativity. We don't learn to control the equilibrium of the mind because, from childhood on, we are trained to use our brain for analytical, everyday processes, rather than for creativity.

We live in a thought world. One lives through one's mind, not one's body: the mind creates reality. Any discord or disharmony that is permitted to exist in the mind is likely to produce an unfortunate effect in the physical body.

About a year ago a very depressed thirty-two-year-old woman came to visit me complaining of lower back pain and a heaviness throughout her pelvic area. I asked her to recall any dramatic traumas from her early childhood, and although reluctant, she eventually related an unhappy story of sexual and physical abuse that had taken place when she was eight years old.

In the course of her examination, I discovered that her life force was blocked in the pelvic area and couldn't flow down through the legs. There her body felt like a rock, a result of the abuse. We worked on her pelvis for about two months, and the process went well; her pain was minimal and she was beginning to enjoy her life again.

Before she felt fully recovered, however, a death occurred in her family. At the funeral parlor the woman took one look at the body of the deceased—the man who had abused her—and all of her symptoms rushed back before she even arrived home that night. Still residing in her were the thought patterns—memories, mental anguish—locked inside the nervous system, blocking the flow of the life force.

She came back to see me the next week, and with more work, we were able to rid her body of her blockages, this time, perhaps, forever.

Every one of us is clothed in our thoughts, and the quality and texture of our energies are woven by the thought patterns we conceive. Thoughts are, indeed, things.

IN SUMMARY

The osteopathic concept of health embraces the harmonious and unrestricted motion of the body and all the body systems.

Breathing is a form of motion, and it is the primary impetus that brings us into existence. Without a full, easy breath, no one can sustain a healthy life. More than an exchange of gases, breath has implications and consequences for the material, mental, and spiritual planes of human existence.

Breath imparts to us a force that is measurable as an electromagnetic field and that we share with all of creation. This field appears both outside of us, as the life field, and inside of us, as the life force.

Every one of us manifests the life force through the vibrations we radiate, each one of us vibrating to an individual frequency. During those times when you don't feel well, your frequency is off.

Trauma can arrest our free breathing and, in turn, will often negatively affect our life force. This can result in pain or disease, although the trauma's full consequences may not be evident until years later.

Thought patterns can also disrupt our breathing and our health, because the constant repetition of negative thoughts will eventually upset the body's chemistry and create restrictions of motion as perilous as those created by physical trauma.

The unimpeded flow of energy is essential for all humans. Therefore the removal of any restriction is the foundation of my work, and if my patients have seen their health improve due to my intervention, this is because I was able to free up the flow of energy in their bodies.

3

Modern Health

Today people talk knowledgeably about medical conditions. I know what's best for that ache, they say, or, I know how to fix that pain—take pills, take exercise, or take a vacation.

They also talk about what's wrong with the medical-care system. The fact that medical costs are very high now is obvious, but there's also an underlying feeling that the practice itself is flawed.

The truth is that modern medicine is facing a crisis, but the reasons behind it may not be quite what you suspect.

WHAT'S WRONG

Not long ago a man appeared at my front door, someone whom I hadn't seen in forty-five years, that being how long ago he had last needed medical help. He had last visited after returning from World War II, when his doctors had said that he was a total wreck, suffering from what they then called nervous exhaustion. It took me just a few sessions to cure the man, improving his condition to the point where he had remained in excellent health for all these decades. Still, he never forgot his experience with osteopathy, which led to his return.

A few weeks prior to his recent visit the man had developed a terrible pain in his chest, and so his doctor sent him to the emergency room. The man ended up spending two full days in the hospital undergoing every imaginable test, yet all the doctors could come up with was a possible infection in his groin area, and they gave him a prescription, which annoyed him, because the drug cost over one hundred dollars and didn't make him feel any better.

That's when he decided to call me for help, and a few days later he was sitting at my house, answering a lengthy series of questions about his medical history, which included details on all his life's activities. At first he seemed surprised by this and said that the doctors at the hospital hadn't asked him much outside of the conventional inquiries concerning his pains. But soon the man relaxed and started talking freely.

Within half an hour he had pretty much related to me the story of his life, but I felt I still hadn't heard enough, so I begged him for more. He looked up at me and said there wasn't much else to tell, except for the fact that he had finally figured out how to stand on his head.

What in the world, I asked, is a seventy-seven-year-old man doing standing on his head?

Oh, he said, I've been practicing yoga for some years now, and that's one of the positions I've mastered.

He didn't see anything wrong with this, so he hadn't mentioned it to anyone.

Now I could guess his problem. He could very well have come out of that position and landed on the ground awkwardly, twisting his neck. So I checked him, and sure enough, there was a problem in his vagus, a nerve located in the neck area that supplies blood to the heart; also his diaphragm was as tight as a board, and I couldn't feel any motion in his head, which indicates a trauma is locked in the body. (This is an area, by the way, that deserves special attention: so often I find that what appears to be heart problems are really nerve problems, and the vagus nerve is a prime trouble spot.)

Through osteopathic manipulation I was able to loosen him up and get the life force flowing again. Afterward he took in a deep breath, let it out, and said that the pain was already disappearing. He then stood up and drove home, and today he reports that his heart hasn't bothered him since.

The unusual part of this story isn't that a seventy-seven-year-old man stood on his head, but that a doctor spent so much time interviewing a patient. Over the last few decades the relationship between doctor and patient has gone sour. Doctors used to be able to spend as many hours with you as they needed to understand the history of your health and then, and only then, to make an informed diagnosis. Now most doctors want you in and out of their office in ten minutes. Sherlock Holmes wouldn't have been able to find out what was wrong with a patient in that amount of time.

Today if doctors do give you more than a few minutes, they may pass along some generic rules and guidelines, such as instructing you to exercise more rigorously or eat less often or sleep more or drink less. They prescribe these things without having any idea how a particular patient might take to exercise or a change in diet, but then they don't have the time to personalize their advice.

When I first started my practice, the medical profession was less restricted, because expenses were lower and the government kept off our backs. We doctors were left on our own to carry on as we saw fit. We practiced as individuals, and our professional work was between us and the patient, and no one else.

Today we practice under many rules and regulations laid down by law. And some of them have been enormously effective in weeding out incompetent doctors and medical practices that did more harm than good. But because so many of these

rules are overly general and impersonal, they eliminate much that is valuable, too. Neither I nor
many of the best doctors I've known could have
worked as we did if we had been forced to deal
with today's regulations, insurance forms, and
peer reviews.

There was a time when doctors could simply
walk into patients' homes, where they were lying
in their own beds in their own bedrooms, and ask
them how they were feeling. They'd give us their
own assessment, and we'd tell them not to worry,
for we'd take care of it all. Just with those words
alone we'd take a huge load off their minds, helping patients start healing immediately, because
they had confidence in us.

Much of the blame for current medical practices
must fall on the system. Doctors operate under
such strict supervision that they can't personalize
their advice for each patient. In some states they
can't even mention alternative medicines without
facing the possibility of losing their license. Mon-
tana legislators have actually passed a law stating
that alternative therapies such as acupuncture or
homeopathy aren't acceptable procedures for li-
censed doctors.

I recently received a letter from a doctor in
northern Ohio who'd just discovered that legislators in Columbus were trying to promote a similar
law eliminating all types of alternative medicine,
right in my own backyard.

To some extent the pharmaceutical companies

encourage these measures, as they certainly don't appreciate the efforts of doctors who warn patients about the ill effects of their drugs.

The insurance business can also shoulder some of the blame for the state of health care. These companies refuse to reimburse patients if doctors don't perform according to their standards, and so most doctors have no choice but to do what the insurer will pay for. How many people know that before doctors consult their books, they may be consulting the patient's insurer?

Even in osteopathy we've been having a difficult time getting the insurance companies to cover our fees, but luckily, due to the American Osteopathic Association's efforts, many of them are coming around.

These days I keep away from insurance entirely. I'd rather give people my treatment than take their insurance.

Another of today's medical problems underscores one of the root differences between osteopathic and allopathic medicine. Allopathic doctors don't want to treat the body as a whole. Instead they insist that the body is composed of individual parts, and thus, by treating those isolated parts alone, they can fix whatever's wrong. This clearly makes no sense; in other scientific disciplines such an approach isn't accepted. Yet in that most sensitive of systems, the human body, doctors have convinced much of the public that each part operates independently and that problems can be addressed without consideration for the rest of the body.

About a year ago a truck driver suffering from terrible back pains showed up at my house for treatment. His route was long and arduous, and when the hydraulic springs in his seat broke while he was driving over some rugged roads, he hurt his back. His company had immediately sent him to an orthopedic surgeon, but he was unable to diagnose the driver's problem and, feeling he had no other options, prescribed painkillers.

The driver then came to me. While I could agree with the orthopedic surgeon that there was nothing obviously wrong with the driver's back—in other words, there was no evidence of a herniated disc or such—I checked out the rest of his body: his legs, his hip socket, his abdomen, his rib cage. Furthermore, instead of looking only for distortion, I was also searching for problems in joint motion, which, we discovered, was exactly what this man was suffering from. By the use of osteopathic manipulation, I was able to free up the trouble, which turned out to be down in his pelvis.

Not long afterward I received a letter from the orthopedic surgeon telling me that my diagnosis couldn't be more wrong and that my work wouldn't help the driver one whit. I wrote back, thanking him for his note, and added that the driver was now quite well. Nor, I found out recently, did his trouble ever return.

ANTIBIOTICS

Have you opened your medicine cabinet and examined what's inside lately? Apart from the mouthwashes and toothpaste and deodorant, it seems you can always find an amber plastic bottle or two, and usually one of them contains some kind of antibiotic. For that matter, when was the last time you went an entire year without a doctor prescribing antibiotics to at least one member of your family?

These days doctors pass out drugs to their patients as though they were harmless candies. But it's the penchant for antibiotics that I find particularly damaging.

Though I believe in the body's own ability to heal itself, this doesn't mean that I'm always against using antibiotics—not at all. In fact, I was one of the first doctors ever to prescribe them in Cincinnati. A physiologist from New York had introduced me to them in the late 1940s during his visit to a local distillery, which was considering their manufacture. At the time, one of my patients was terminally ill, and so I told him about the new drugs and the physiologist's request that I find a volunteer to try them. The patient agreed because both of us felt the alternative was probably death. The antibiotics performed well, and it wasn't long before the patient had regained his strength.

When a doctor diagnoses a patient with a disease and then prescribes a drug to treat it, the patient immediately thinks that the drug will help; this can replace the old pattern of thought—I'm very sick—with a new one: I'm going to get well. So by helping the patient think the healing process is going to take place, the recuperative processes commence.

But drugs, and particularly antibiotics, aren't the right answer for every ailment. For instance, the normal treatment for children's otitis media, or earaches, is a two-to-three-month course of antibiotics. A better remedy might be for doctors to figure out what's actually causing the problem.

Most doctors use antibiotics because they view the ear infection as taking place solely within the ear itself. But the problem actually starts at the child's birth, when a recto-respiratory reflex affects the lymphatic drainage in the neck and the upper part of the shoulder. Thus it's not the ear that needs the treatment, but the entire body. My solution is to loosen up the pelvis as well as the rib cage, which gets that lymphatic fluid flowing through the system, and then put some glycerin drops in each ear. The otitis media should then clear up.

Because I was having so much success with this treatment, and because so many medical doctors thought it wasn't possible, some people at the University of Arizona decided to videotape me treating a child suffering from one of these infections. So, while the cameras rolled, I worked on the boy as

I normally do, and the treatment was successful enough that even the boy's pediatrician eventually admitted, after six months had passed, that the child hadn't had an ear infection since, although before, he had been averaging one every six weeks.

Over the years I've treated hundreds of children this way, and nearly all of them improved without the ill effects of drugs.

The problem with antibiotics isn't limited to their unnecessary use. Antibiotics are, I suspect, indirectly responsible for the public's basic lack of concern about their personal health. When World War II ended, medical doctors returned to America loaded with these drugs, all the while telling people that medicine had finally invented a wonder pill that would take care of any illness at all. People believed their doctors and stopped paying as much attention to their own welfare. Why worry, when the cure for everything was easy, available, and relatively inexpensive?

It turned out, however, that bacteria in the body continually builds up a resistance to antibiotics, which in turn forces doctors to increase the dosage. Eventually the antibiotics won't work, as is the case with certain kinds of strep bacteria that are now resistant to current drugs: chemists and physiologists are trying to find new antibiotics to take their place.

No one knows exactly what type of damage may be caused by taking too many antibiotics, but is their liberal use worth the risk? One man who studied the effects of these pills in animals told me he could determine what happens to seventy percent of an antibiotic by tracking its course through the body, but he had no idea where the other thirty percent went over the long term. My own guess is that the drugs could be breaking down the immune system, since they would be suppressing symptoms for so long.

This suppressive aspect of antibiotics is also of questionable value. When you have an infection of some kind, such as pneumonia, you're prescribed antibiotics to suppress the disease, rather than allow the pneumonia to progress through its normal stage of development and recession; the result is temporary relief, but the strong possibility exists that the illness may flare up again someday, in some other form, such as arthritis.

Nowadays if you come down with a fever, the first thing you're told to do is rid yourself of it. In my osteopathic college we were told the opposite—to encourage the body to react to whatever was trying to manifest itself by developing a fever. A fever up to 103 degrees Fahrenheit can be good for you. Your body is continually burning up waste materials in the form of cells, which are constantly in the process of dying. If these cells can't leave your body in a normal pattern, they'll start to accumulate, and so Mother Nature creates a fever to incinerate the dead cells and restore the disposal process. A fever may be exactly what your body needs.

Whenever you can, avoid antibiotics. If you have a fever below 103, no drug may be appropriate. Yes, sometimes these drugs are necessary to keep the body alive: I myself wouldn't be here without them, nor would millions of other Americans. But if you truly want to heal, you have to nourish the entire being, and the best way you can do that is through alternative medicines that work with the life force, such as acupuncture or herbs or osteo-pathic manipulation.

PROGRESS

Today we live in a world proud to consider itself scientific. Everything has to be proven by science before it can be accepted, and to prove anything, science has to first split the matter into parts and then proceed to prove each of these parts, ad infi-nitum. I've seen specialists who've become so in-volved in what they're doing that they have forgotten there's more to the body than, for in-stance, the left knee joint.

As this fragmented process continues, and the media report on the results of this trial and that experiment and some other test, the public be-comes so engrossed with all this research into the individual parts that they, too, forget about the wholeness within themselves.

We—doctors and patients both—must all get back to that wholeness. The parts are important, certainly, but it won't be of any use to understand the individual elements if you don't comprehend the entire picture. There is more to the world than a statistician's bell-shaped curve.

This illusion of progress has infected osteopathy as well. As mentioned earlier, osteopathic schools in the last few decades have lessened their emphasis on manipulation, and those examinations with bones wrapped up in blankets to test a student's sense of touch have fallen out of favor. Instead, emphasis on drug therapy has increased, just as it has in allopathic medicine. In other words, today some osteopaths are probably not much different from allopaths.

But things are beginning to change once more, because the public is getting fed up with modern doctors. People want to be treated by someone who is attentive and caring, not distant and hurried. There's also a growing understanding that the mind and the body are related and that viewing the two separately doesn't make much sense.

The best sign of real progress is that osteopathic manipulation is making a comeback. Dr. Elmer Green, director emeritus at the Voluntary Controls Program at the Menninger Clinic in Topeka, Kansas, has said that alternative medicine can handle about seventy percent of all the visits people pay to a medical doctor. Certainly one of those alternative medicines includes manipulation, and while manipulation may have skipped a generation of osteopaths, many of the students in school today are learning about it once more. So perhaps progress isn't as simple as it seems, for what might look like a step forward to one person is a step backward to another.

4

Improving Modern Health

If we want to improve the state of modern health, we must recognize and treat the deeper, but usually unconsidered, causes of illness. This chapter will explain some of these deeper causes and describe how the alternative power of osteopathy addresses them.

TRAUMA

There is one particular medical problem that few doctors ever consider when they examine their patients. It's one that I feel can make all the difference in the world between well-being and ill health.

This problem is trauma.

When your life force is jammed, your breath won't flow well through your body, and that can cause a general decline in your health.

The primary cause of this blockage is trauma, and by that I mean any major, damaging psychological or physical event that has occurred during your life.

For many people, that first trauma relates to their birth. There are no exact figures as to how often trauma takes place during delivery, but from my practice I've noticed it's a remarkably high percentage.

Birth is one of the more convoluted natural human experiences. As I've said, in order to get through that birth canal, the child has to be squeezed, crushed, twisted, and compressed, and the baby's first cry goes a long way to help unlock that squeezed position and reset the entire bony structure.

In the old days, before the advent of this country's love affair with lawsuits, the accepted medical procedure was to take the baby, grab it by the ankles, and give it a good whack on the rear end. That shot caused the child to let out a terrific whoop, which in turn allowed air to rush into its body.

Today, you'd be sued for that kind of behavior. Instead doctors take their thumbs and lightly tap the bottom of the baby's foot. This is somewhat effective, but it's nowhere near as effective as that slap and cry.

During the mid 1950s, the celebrated French obstetrician Dr. Frederick LeBoyer came to this country to lecture on the delivery process. Dr. LeBoyer had devised what I feel is the best procedure for delivering a baby. The umbilical cord, he said, must not be cut until the last pulsation from the mother. The child should then be immediately placed in a bath of water up to its neck, reminding the child of its first home—the womb—therefore causing it to relax. At that point the doctor puts his hands underneath the baby, bringing it slowly up out of the water. If the baby tightens, the doctor returns it to the water, and then tries again, until he can finally raise that child into the air without its bursting into tears in fear of its new environment.

Babies delivered using this method have turned out to be excellent, healthy specimens. I recently examined one of them, a child who had been delivered by the father while the mother was in a bathtub filled with water; the father cut the cord at the appropriate time. The only reason the parents came to see me was to ensure that the baby was in good health, since they were afraid to tell a pediatrician the child had been delivered underwater.

Dr. LeBoyer visited my office in Cincinnati twice, and we were happy to discover that we agreed completely. That doesn't happen to me very often.

Another of the great experts on childbirth is Henry M. Truby, PhD, whose book, *The Baby's Cry*, is one of the most important ever written on the subject. In his native Sweden, Dr. Truby completed a study of 1,500 sound spectographic analyses, recording the moment of the child's first cry, and followed up with studies of those children through their first seven years of maturation. In doing so, he was able to obtain a pattern of the growth and development of each child's personality.

After assimilating his results, Dr. Truby declared that he could determine, from the baby's very first breath or cry, that particular baby's personality, its weaknesses, and the degree of its health and well-being. The first breath, Dr. Truby argues, surely predicts everything.

Another study from Sweden worth mentioning is one of 412 patients in six Stockholm hospitals, all born before 1940, who died of the effects of drug addiction and alcoholism or suicide between 1978 and 1984. The researchers found that, more than any other risk factor for which they tested, it was birth trauma that was most closely associated with suicide.

Even more persuasive is the work of Bertil Jacobson, head of the Department of Medical Engineering at Karolensha Institute in Sweden, who has spent a lifetime researching associations between prenatal experience and adolescent events.

According to Dr. Jacobson's studies, suicide was more closely associated with birth trauma than with any of the other eleven risk factors for which he tested (including such socioeconomic variables as parental alcoholism and broken homes). In addition, Dr. Jacobson's results indicate a strong correlation between the type of trauma suffered at birth and the method by which suicide or violent death occurred during adolescence. Two thousand nine hundred cases of suicide by asphyxiation were closely associated with some form of asphyxiation at birth. For those who killed themselves using some form of mechanical procedure, the researchers found many had experienced mechanical trauma at birth—for instance, the use of forceps or other metal instruments to help deliver the baby. And drug addiction among the suicide victims had a high correlation to administration of opiates and barbiturates during labor.

And, in a 1985 study published in the British medical journal *Lancet,* psychologist Lee Salk of Cornell University Medical School also encountered strong links between birth trauma and suicide in adolescents. Three common denominators were detected in his study: (1) respiratory distress in excess of one hour at birth; (2) lack of proper prenatal care before the twentieth week of pregnancy; (3) chronic ill health of the mother during her pregnancy.

Problems related to birth trauma are endemic to our society. I already mentioned the boy who recently came to see me after spending his first four years being uncontrollably wild. Another recent case was that of a three-week-old child whose father, an allopathic physician, had noticed that the boy was breathing poorly, almost as though he were snorting instead of inhaling. In desperation the father called me and asked if I would work with his son.

A preliminary examination of the child showed me that he had very limited motion in his rib cage and his pelvis. Using my percussion vibrator (which is described later in this chapter), I gave the child a figurative spanking on his bottom and then went to work on his skull. After thirty minutes the boy abruptly let out a great big war whoop, and then we laid him back down on the table and watched as his breath slowly returned. The father tells me the child hasn't had a problem since.

Here's another case. About five years ago I saw a young boy who had been diagnosed as hyperactive and convulsive, totally baffling his neurologist, who could find nothing amiss despite repeated examinations.

I saw the boy for one session, and all I did was release his skull so it was able to expand, because when he was born he didn't get that good first breath to spread it apart on its own.

Soon afterward his mother sent me a letter telling me of the boy's progress. Within one day she noticed that for the first time in his life he was listening carefully to conversations and had been able to sit down and complete his homework without running all over the house. She added that she had brought the boy in to see his neurologist a week after my session, and the boy's head circumference had grown by one half a centimeter since his last examination. The doctor was impressed, although startled, by the changes.

Eventually the boy did well enough in class to leave his school for the mentally handicapped and enroll in a local public school.

Throughout my career, whenever I see a patient, I always ask for as detailed a history of birth as the parents can remember. Unfortunately, millions of children started off their lives without that good first breath, and I'm one of them. I've been working on myself all my life to correct that and have discovered so many things in my body: a twisted left knee, a tight rib cage, a left shoulder that's just beginning to straighten itself out. My problem was that I didn't start working on myself until I was over forty years old, and from my experience with patients, I've learned that the older you are, the more difficult it is to take out the kinks from your system.

If you can, find out the state of your breath when you were born; if you have an osteopath who works the way I do, the information can be very useful. And if you're thinking about having children, watch them as they appear. By paying attention to that first breath, we can help change the state of the world's health.

NONBIRTH TRAUMA

I wish I had the time to describe where all the various kinds of trauma can show up in the human body, because if I did, I could alert people to problem areas. But since trauma can lodge itself in the body in so many different situations, it would require volumes to record them all. There are some general tendencies, however.

Most nonbirth traumas occur near the home and often in commonplace circumstances. For instance, it's startling how many times in the last few years I've had to work with infants who'd been placed in one of those metal shopping carts in supermarkets and, once left on their own, started pushing the carts with their feet. The next thing you knew, they'd gone right down the stairs or fallen onto the floor or managed to crash into a display.

Trauma takes place on ice skates and in wagons, on stairs and in messy garages, on basketball courts and in shopping malls. I can think of few places where it wouldn't be possible to hurt yourself.

But trauma isn't just physiological: psychological traumas can be equally injurious. A death in the family, a separation, a divorce—once people fall into a grieving state, they may not snap out of it. Every time they think of the person who passed on or is in some way separated from them, they slip right back into that grieving pattern. They end up in a deep depression, because they didn't allow themselves to go through a good three-month grieving period and then let the past settle itself into the memory for good.

Why is this so harmful? Because such a pattern finds its way into the nervous system and upsets the entire body chemistry. And its damaging effect can manifest itself anywhere, in many syndromes, from stomach cramps to cataracts. Sometimes I think the body's internal systems resemble those long domino arrangements, where if you knock down one tile, it knocks down the next, and that knocks down the next, and so on.

Unfortunately, I myself am a good example of this process. That doctor mentioned in the Prologue, the one who had suffered congestive heart failure after his wife developed Alzheimer's disease, is me. Two years of taking care of my wife had exhausted me to the point of complete vulnerability. But in a sense, the heart failure served me well, for it was a reminder that no one is immune from their negative thoughts, even those of us who try to stay aware of their implications. Thoughts are indeed things, and I have become ever more heedful to observe my mind.

Because our culture teaches us so little about the connection between the body and the mind, few of us stop to realize that our physical ailments can arise from mental distress. I can't tell you how many times patients come to see me complaining of various physical ailments, when I'm convinced that they're actually suffering from psychological trauma.

For instance, one woman in her early fifties sought me out last year because, for over twenty years, she had been tormented by terrible back pains and high fevers. The official diagnosis was gallstones, although no doctor could prove this. During the course of a lengthy conversation, I discovered that her relationships with her father and her sister had been filled with suffering. It's my belief that the pain in her back resulted from this family distress. Emotional distress almost always finds a way to manifest itself as physical pain, anywhere from the head to the foot.

I told the woman that if she could resolve this emotional torment, her physical health would change, but she refused to believe me. To this day she still visits me for relief of her pain, but refuses to deal with her emotions. Few people are willing to admit that their mind could be responsible for physical problems when it's much easier to place the blame on someone or something else.

It's unfortunately true that many of us don't recover from the psychological effects of childhood. Consider the parental approval-disapproval syndrome, or the situation that arises whenever your father says no and your mother says yes simultaneously. There you are in the formative years of your childhood, developing your first relationships with the world, and you can't get a clear message from the people who mean the most to you.

Let's say you want to take a break from your homework. Dad says you can't, that you have to finish before you go outside. Mom says a little exercise and freedom might do you some good and encourages you to leave. Over the long run these kinds of conflicts create a drag on the emotional system; they upset the body's chemistry and later in life generate genuine physical pain. I can feel this with my hands: The majority of people have a reflex center in the sternum, or the breastbone, where the body's deep-seated emotional patterns tend to collect. When I'm not able to find any motion there, I'm just about one hundred percent certain that an emotional lock is taking place in the body—some major psychological issue hasn't been resolved.

Another woman who's been seeing me is in severe pain and has been diagnosed with myalgia—an inflammation of the muscle tissues. The problem goes back to her early childhood and the difficulties she had with her parents. Whenever she starts to make a decision today, that same struggle that took place so many years ago between her mother and her father occurs inside her head. I can feel this in her breastbone.

While I always try to understand their personal histories, I avoid becoming overly involved in my patients' emotional lives, because that's a therapist's business. But over the years I've found that there are quite a number of patients who, once I get that sternum loosened up, feel as much emotional as physical relief.

I've seldom instructed patients to consult a therapist, but when I have, I never once claimed that such a professional would relieve a patient's physical pain. A doctor shouldn't make that kind of a broad statement, because the force of powerful expectations can stop patients from feeling at ease when they talk to someone else. The most I might say is that I was sorry, I had done as much as I could, and that as far as I could observe, the patient could benefit from a conversation with a counselor, perhaps, or a minister.

There have been times, however, when I've felt obliged to offer at least some guidance concerning my patients' emotional lives. One exercise I've often recommended is to sit at a desk in a darkened room before bedtime and write out your life history, going backward in time. Most people can't write their history starting from day one; they remember more by starting with the present and slowly unpeeling each layer of memory. That's why I recommend the backward technique.

When a page becomes full, throw it on the floor without reading it and start on a new page. Then, when you've exhausted yourself for the night, take all those pages, put a match to them, and watch them burn away. Do this as often as you need.

In my experience, this exercise brings up those thought patterns that have been stored in the recesses of our brain and that may still be disturbing the body's metabolism. One of my most unusual cases was a young woman who had no control over the motion of her head; it continuously wobbled back and forth, like a toy. Although she had sought out medical help from many different doctors, no one could help. Neither, it turned out when she came to me, could I. So, for lack of anything else, I asked her to try the above exercise.

Being conscientious, the woman faithfully wrote several pages of her life story every week, even though she didn't detect any progress. Then, one evening, she asked her husband to prepare dinner alone, for the urge to go upstairs and write had overcome her. Once in her bedroom she wrote down the same words over and over: I can't, I can't, I can't. I can't.

After burning the pages as always, she returned to the kitchen. There she seemed so different that her husband couldn't comprehend the drastic change. Although we'll never know for sure, those words probably referred to some experience in her childhood, a response to somebody who was requesting her to perform some act that her inner self refused. That shaking of her head expressed the negative emotion involved, and once she had written those words down on paper, her symptoms disappeared.

If you're having physical problems, don't underestimate the need to explore your emotional life as well.

ANNIVERSARIES OF PAIN

The other day I woke up feeling a little under the weather. But I rose anyway and decided to get myself something to eat, because I was feeling hungry. I took a teaspoonful of cottage cheese, sat down, and about five minutes later I had a vomiting spell so violent it felt as if my gut was spilling out of me. A few hours later I tried to drink some water and had the same experience, so I ended up not taking in any food or water all that day.

I didn't know what was wrong until my doctor telephoned to inquire about my health. I told him what had happened, but wondered why he had asked. It's now a year since your heart failure, he said, and you know what happens on anniversaries of pain.

Of course, he was right. Over the last fifty years I've found it amazing how these anniversaries pop up. This is my first personal experience, but I've seen it in others countless times as a doctor. So often when my patients were curious why they'd come down with something out of the blue, I'd check their files and tell them about their anniversary, and they'd say, oh, yes, I forgot about that.

An anniversary of an illness can make you recall the past memory of your pain and the details of your life since then, the bad as well as the good. Something about this process is weakening.

This syndrome varies widely: many people never feel it at all, others feel it so slightly that they may never be aware of the connection to their earlier illness. Some come down with minor symptoms of whatever had attacked them on this date before, and there are those, like myself, who become quite ill.

No one has a clue why this happens, but it's my guess that traumas get imprinted either in the nervous system or in the muscles. The morning of my anniversary I may have made one move that triggered that memory in one of those two places, and that was all my system needed.

Such an anniversary can take place one year later, or four, or ten. Familiarize yourself with these dates, so that, if you do become ill, you can check a calendar quickly and prevent yourself from becoming too concerned. And that in itself can make things easier to bear.

A TYPICAL SESSION

Now that we've seen the way trauma, both major and minor, can compromise our health, let's look at how osteopathic treatment can handle these problems. Let me first introduce you to my own technique.

Although I officially retired in my mid-eighties, people still seek me out. I don't know how to say no to a child who needs help. And frankly, I seldom turn down adults, either, if I think my service could be beneficial.

The following describes how one of my sessions used to work when I was practicing full-time. Except for the presence of an assistant, it's not unlike how I work today.

When patients arrived in my Cincinnati office,

my assistant greeted them at the front desk and wrote down their case histories, along with their addresses and telephone numbers, their ages, and the time they were born.

I then read each history in my office, alone, and became as familiar as I could be with the patient before he or she entered the examining room. No one ever repeats word for word what they've written, so I would then ask for the same information, and the discrepancies between the two versions were often illuminating.

Because I believe that energy flows into the body in the morning and out in the afternoon (see Chapter 5), I like to learn the time of day my patients were born, because I must work harder for those born in the evening. There were no birth certificates in 1905, but I would guess that my own birth took place in the morning, since I have a good deal of energy then.

If the patient was female, I had to ask permission to put my hands upon her body—otherwise I could have landed in trouble, especially with the young. And occasionally people did refuse, in which case I'd say that I was sorry, but that I couldn't work with them without touch. Often they then changed their minds, because most people came to me after a good recommendation from a former patient.

My method of examining the body hasn't changed greatly in the last several decades. I inspect it from the bottom of the feet to the top of the head, checking the motion of all the joints, always looking for restrictions in the joint surfaces—in other words, trying to locate places in the body where the life force isn't flowing.

The movement I'm looking for is a reaction to what osteopaths call a subtle motion: there's a significant difference between that and gross motion. With the latter you can make almost anything move, but I don't learn anything from pushing a joint with force. A light touch to the joint, and the joint's response, tells me what I need to know.

First I look at the feet, and then the ankle joints. Do they have a normal range of extension? Or is the movement restricted, meaning that when the patient walks, the feet don't have that rhythmic balance that should always be present? That can throw the pelvis out of alignment, which in turn can upset the position of the diaphragm.

After the ankles, I move up the legs to the knees, from where I can tell if the pelvis is well-balanced—a bad knee also throws the pelvis out of line.

I examine the rotation of the leg and hip socket, and then the pelvis itself: is it in line or does it have a torsion, or twist, in the bony structure? If the pelvis isn't functioning properly, then organs from the kidneys to the bladder may not be receiving a proper blood supply.

I look at the abdomen. If it's bloated, that might mean a bad diet, which severely affects the body chemistry. I feel for bloating by pressing down my hands to check for resistance, just as the only way to diagnose an acute appendicitis in the 1940s, was to feel it through the skin.

I search for motion in the diaphragm. The diaphragm isn't working well in a high percentage of patients because so many have had their breath knocked out at some point in their life. A bad diaphragm can block the amount of air getting into the nervous system.

I look to see if the rib cage is moving well on both sides. If it isn't, this could mean that one of the lungs isn't functioning at its best.

Then the arms: can the patient raise them to a full 180 degree angle? If not, that would mean there's a restriction of the rib motion, which could disturb the respiration on that side of the body.

I check to see if the head moves easily from side to side, or if the chin will rotate more toward one shoulder than the other. If so, this may mean one of the vertebrae in the neck is out of line in relationship to the opposite side, and that could disturb the blood supply into the brain, which could create any number of problems, including, for instance, a migraine headache.

Also important is the motion of the skull bones and whether both hemispheres of the brain are in motion. To check this I lay my palm on one side of the head, and then I use the other palm to compare what I feel on the opposite side, which gives me a clue if both the hemispheres are in equal motion.

For many years the osteopathic assumption of

cranial bone motion was considered by allopaths to be a mark of our lack of understanding. The skull doesn't move! the medical doctors used to retort. However, recent research at Michigan State University has proved that, indeed, a subtle movement does take place in the skull.

It's a wonderful sensation to place your hands on a healthy person's head, because it feels as though that head is going to float out from underneath your hands, the movement is so clear and rhythmic. This is one of the body's key areas, the place from where the nervous system originates, and the lack of movement here could indicate severe headaches or a disturbance in the sleep pattern or something more serious. In children it often indicates a learning disability, because limited movement implies limited circulation, and so the brain cells won't be getting the chance to develop properly. (In the early 1950s I received permission to work at a school for learning-impaired students, treating a group of ten children five days a week for three months. At the end of the experiment, the average child's IQ had increased from approximately 80 to over 100.)

Let's say I do find a problem—for instance, perhaps the left knee has a torsion, or a twist; the joint isn't lining up properly. I then take out my percussion vibrator, which is composed of a motor, a flexible shaft, and a head piece with an applicator that holds a rubber pad two and a half inches in diameter, and use it to massage the body. This will relax the tension in the ligaments and the muscle attached around the knee joint. Then we put the joint through its range of motion; this brings it up, straightens it out again, and allows the joint to normalize itself.

The percussion vibrator was originally invented for use as a massage tool. I started using it during World War II, soon after I had opened my practice along with eight medical doctors. A year later, only two medical doctors and myself were left in the office, and the three of us were working far too hard. At that point I was using my hands to massage the muscles along my patients' spinal column and finding this too time-consuming. One day a folder arrived in the mail advertising this percussion vibrator, and I knew immediately it could save me much time, allowing me to loosen up muscles without overexertion. The company that makes the vibrator was quite surprised to discover that osteopaths were using it for medical purposes; eventually they tailor-made a smaller, more practical version for us.

I never use the percussion vibrator on a child without letting the mother or father feel it first, so that they are fully comfortable with the machine.

Perhaps I notice a restriction in a patient's skull: I place my hands very lightly on the head, with the hands in normal polarity—the right hand on the left side of the head and the left hand on the right side. The forces running between my hands set up a rhythm in the brain that begins to move the skull. I use no coercion whatsoever.

That movement in the skull should be palpable. As I work on the head, the patient feels that tingling sensation as we open up the nervous system and allow the brain to find its natural rhythm. The body then begins to normalize itself.

When a session ends, I often show patients how their bodies may have changed: perhaps they can now raise their arms more easily or the rotary motion in their pelvis has improved. Almost all of them notice what a good, deep breath they can now take.

My patients also frequently comment on a strange feeling that flows over them after being manipulated—a pleasant, tingling sensation that can surface throughout their whole body. What they're feeling is the life force, which was once blocked and is now surging again.

Generally I then suggest some sort of exercise that I feel a particular patient might need.

Many patients come in for a single session, although I often ask them to return in three months for a checkup and also to ensure that they're doing all the exercises I've prescribed. Other patients may visit more frequently, and there are a few who have come in to see me year after year—but some of these, I fear, don't need me as much as they enjoy the manipulation.

People often ask me what I'm thinking while my hands are moving over the body. The answer is, at best, nothing. I have no thoughts. I'm trying to observe and comprehend the patient's life force through touch, and my own thoughts could distort my findings. If I'm not able to intepret what I feel in my hands quickly and without prejudice, the procedure won't succeed.

INTUITION

Intuition is an important element in osteopathy, and one that's missing from modern medicine. For me it comes into play in numerous cases and is, in fact, a major reason why I'm able to resolve so many unusual ailments. I can't explain intuition logically: it's not a voice in my head, nor is it words on the wall or writing in the sky. It's just an inexplicable feeling, one that somehow leads me toward accurate diagnoses.

My sense is that outstanding physicians from the Greek physician Hippocrates on have invariably relied on their intuition. But medical doctors can't admit this, because today every diagnosis has to come from what an instrument tells you or what a machine predicts or what a textbook instructs, instead of what intuition says. But it is a strong part of medicine and always has been.

ATTITUDE

A doctor's beliefs will always affect the patient.
Until patients break down the old pattern of

thought—that they're ill—and establish a new one—that they're going to get better—the healing processes can't start. And who better to help that good pattern develop than a doctor?

Whereas the public might once have scoffed at such a notion, today it's fairly well accepted. You'd never know this, though, by observing doctors practice. Instead of encouraging patients to feel secure and well attended, it's as if they were trying to convey an attitude of thoughtlessness.

For some doctors, this negative attitude derives from dissatisfaction with their practice. And if a doctor's attitude toward his practice isn't positive, his attitude toward his patients will be poor. If that in turn is true, he's not going to have a prosperous practice, either, which will probably make him angrier. It's a bad cycle that many professionals can't shake.

A friend once told me that a doctor has only four minutes in which to succeed or fail in his relationship with a patient. So the doctor's attitude and appearance upon entering the room, along with the first questions and conversation, are all of utmost importance.

One aspect of this quick judgment process is the doctor's office itself. It must be an inviting place. Back when I ran an office in Cincinnati, our waiting room was usually full, but often not with waiting patients. People used to come in even when they didn't have an appointment, just to sit in a restful haven. After a while, feeling more calm, they'd leave.

The other day a doctor who's setting up shop in Cincinnati called and asked me to tell him the key to success. I said the answer was love for other human beings. If you can't project that love, I said, you're not going to be able to help anyone.

Patients benefit from doctors' loving attitude in several ways. When doctors project the sense of confidence that comes from that love, patients will reflect that confidence back to their doctors. And when this occurs, patients build up faith—not belief. (I say faith, and not belief, because belief comes from the mind, from mental activities, whereas faith arises out of the person's spiritual side, out of the natural purity of the spiritual body, which starts the healing process in motion immediately.)

There are times when I'm working with patients, particularly children, that I feel as though I've become a part of them. Unlike most doctors, I'm not sitting across a desk, watching from a distance and barking out orders. One of the most wonderful aspects of osteopathy is our close contact with patients. And because we touch and move our hands over the body and manipulate the bony structure until we return it to its rightful place, we become a tangible component of the healing process.

The projection of love doesn't guarantee results, however. Some patients resist close contact. Some make the work too difficult. Some are just impossible. Once I was treating a thirteen-year-old boy while his mother was watching, frowning and tapping her foot until she finally yelled, Dr. Fulford, you better be doing that right or we're going to have to sue you!

I knew immediately that this kind of talk had taken place in front of the boy at home, before he ever arrived at the office. I was in a terrible predicament. The boy's healing powers were difficult to reach, since his attitude had been poisoned. But I just went on with my work and didn't pay any attention to his mother's shouts or comment on them. If I had, I would have exaggerated the problem; by not saying a word, the problem was voided.

Occasionally I've been forced to send some people away. One mother, watching me treat her child, shrieked that everything I was doing was wrong. Her cries penetrated my entire office, so that all the patients in the waiting room had to hear them, too. Why should I have someone around who's disturbing everyone else? I'm sorry, I said, I cannot treat your son, you'll have to find another doctor. And I walked out of the room, because it seemed the best way to save the others.

TOUCH

Oftentimes my patients enter my office in pain, sobbing. I start their treatment immediately by giving them a tissue, encouraging them to cry or talk, and putting my hands on their head. It's remarkable how much relief that one simple act can bestow and how rapidly patients quiet down. Touch is a marvelous and neglected gift.

See how a mother takes care of her baby: she puts her loving hand upon its feverish brow, or she'll hold the child in her arms, giving quiet comfort. The baby will often grow calm in response to this touch alone.

Hippocrates found that, when treating his patients, healing power radiated from his hands, about which he wrote: "It has often appeared, while I have been soothing a patient, as if there were some strange property in my hands to pull and draw away from the afflicted parts aches and diverse impurities by laying my hands upon the place of discomfort."

I have often felt the same way. Sometimes, while I've been soothing the patient, it has seemed as though some strange property occupied my hands, too.

Few medical doctors use this art of touch enough, and that means that they're losing close and restorative contact with the patient. When most doctors use their hands today, it's to scribble out a prescription. This is such a sad waste of human potential.

Another seldom considered aspect of touch is polarity.

I believe the body to be electric, and every electric field has a positive and a negative side. If you place a magnet's negative edge next to another magnet's negative edge, they'll repel each other. If they're aligned properly with each other, negative to positive, they'll attract.

The same is true for people. The minister after his Sunday sermon who tries to shake hands with everyone who approaches him finds that, when he goes home, he's got a dead hand, because a profusion of right-hand-to-right-hand shakes can be brutal. The minister can avoid that numbness if he uses both hands to grasp the hands of the other person.

I can't even imagine how a politician must feel after attending rally after rally for years, and I wonder how much our political system might improve if politicians only paid more attention to the facts of the human body.

Few doctors are taught about the proper polarity of hands in relationship to the body. (This applies only to the sensory portion of the human body, or the front side, and not the body's motor section, or the back.) As a result, diagnoses are often botched. For instance, if I put my right hand on the right rib cage, I will get very little give. But when I put my left hand over the right rib cage, I find a spring to the ribs. We mislead ourselves if we take our right hand and push on the patient's right chest wall and assume from the response that there is abnormal motion in the rib cage. If doctors don't use the proper pairing of their hands, they will get an abnormal response and mar their diagnosis.

⇐ 5 ⇒

Take Good Care of Yourself

Health care today is flawed, and both practioners and the public suffer from this. But there are avenues other than traditional medicine that can lead you to better health.

The principles I've outlined so far can be of value, because once you've embraced these ideas, you may well find yourself investigating new options. One place you might consider starting to look is inside yourself, where you may find more help than you ever imagined.

WILL YOURSELF TO WELLNESS

Osteopaths believe that the body wants to be well. After all, the spiritual being in all of us is healthy (see Chapter 7). And it wants to express itself in the material world through a good, healthy body.

Perhaps people will take better care of what they have, once they realize that their natural state is one of well-being rather than infirmity.

Look at burn victims. Somehow these individuals are able to generate new tissue to replace their old, burned skin. Medicine has never been able to reproduce that effort: it can graft new skin onto the body, but it can't create what the body can regenerate naturally.

Or look at the eastern yogis who can manifest physical reactions in their bodies using only their will—but these people meditate as much as ten hours a day. It's going to be some time before westerners are willing to devote that kind of energy to the spiritual—and experience those kinds of extraordinary results.

The problem in western culture is that too many people fall prey to their desires, desires that impede the will to reach health.

I had a patient who suffered from severe headaches. The first doctors he sought out knew of no way to cure him other than prescribing enormous amounts of narcotics. These drugs did indeed alleviate the man's pain, but were eventually so addictive that by the time he saw me, he wouldn't stop taking them, even though my manipulation eased his pain equally well. My guess is that, despite sensing that the painkillers actually hurt him, he won't ever stop taking them, because his desire for the narcotic high is greater than his will to get well.

I have another patient who's an avid soccer player. This young man originally visited me because he was born with his left foot in a twist—the result of coming out of the womb in a bad position—and the doctors put a cast on it to strengthen it out. This didn't cure anything, although it did ease the pain.

Many years later the boy hurt himself in his pelvic area while playing soccer. The sports doctors couldn't help, so they brought him back to me.

Using manipulation we were able to straighten out the pain in his pelvis, and yet the boy keeps hurting himself and returning to me. Why? Because he insists on playing soccer. The boy's desire to play has overwhelmed his will to stay healthy.

Another patient of mine from Oklahoma visits me twice a year. She first came a decade ago, complaining about stiffness in the right side of her pelvis. It turned out that at the age of eight she fell off a horse, and a few years later she hurt herself skating. The injuries she received from those accidents had never really been addressed.

Now I've done everything I can for this woman, and as far as I can tell, her body is in fine shape. Every time she leaves me she tells me she never felt better. But then she calls me again in a few months with the same complaints. She just doesn't want to let go of that thought pattern, because her desire to complain and think of herself as injured is far greater than her will to be well.

Thankfully, desire can work the other way, too. Another patient, a talented young artist, first came to see me in a wheelchair. During her early twenties she had become paralyzed from the waist down, and had developed restricted movement in her hands as well. Her doctor couldn't help, because he couldn't discover what was wrong.

After examining the woman, I, too, felt confused until I suddenly asked her how much coffee she drank. Fourteen cups a day, she answered, and wondered why I had asked—no one ever had before. I told her that she might be suffering from caffeine poisoning, and if so, that the caffeine was inhibiting the normal functioning of her nervous system. The woman then decided, although she loved coffee, never to touch it again. Within a week she proved the accuracy of my diagnosis by being able to walk into the office, and today her paralysis has totally vanished. (This doesn't mean that too much coffee will paralyze you, too. Some people can drink twenty cups a day with no harm; it depends on you. Few rules apply to every body.)

Instead of thinking to yourself, what a poor fish I am, tell yourself that you're on the road to health. It can't hurt you to attempt to influence your desire, and in my experience, it can help considerably.

WHAT TO LOOK FOR IN A DOCTOR

I can't emphasize enough that you must commit yourself to your own health. And that means consciously making decisions about what's best for you, personally.

Given all the recent changes in the health-care system, it's increasingly difficult to give advice concerning doctor-patient relationships, for example. People no longer have simple options, and choosing your own doctor, once considered common, is now something of an indulgence. For the most part, Health Maintenance Organizations (HMOs) are replacing the old family doctor.

But HMOs are highly problematic. Rather than imparting a sense of warm and personal attention, this system turns you into a number. You may lose the valuable feeling that someone cares, because you may be forced to see a doctor you didn't personally choose, or you may see different doctors over a period of time. Not that these doctors aren't skilled, but they probably just don't have the time to study your case as they should.

HMOs are primarily concerned with wealth, not health. Their philosophy is, if we can invest our money and earn a nice thirteen percent from it, doesn't that make for a good procedure? They're not concerned with the actual service they provide. How can they be if each physician is given less than ten minutes to spend with a patient?

The system is complicated, and medical care is costly, but does an HMO have to be the only answer? I tell people to change the system. Rebel! Instead of surrendering to an HMO, try seeking out alternative care. Remember Dr. Elmer Green's remark that about seventy percent of all visits to medical doctors can be handled by alternative medicine. Next time that you feel the need to enter the medical system, consider the alternatives. Does a visit to an uncaring stranger who's as likely as not to give you a handful of drugs that don't truly help seem like a smart idea?

There are occasions, however, when a medical doctor is the right choice. And many careful and thoughtful doctors are still practicing.

When it's time to find such a physician, you should keep certain considerations in mind if events allow you to select your own.

For one, where did you get the doctor's name? Did it come from a friend whose opinion you respect who had a good experience with that doctor? Is the doctor's reputation solid throughout the community? A "yes" answer to these questions can help to set up the proper positive attitude before your first visit, so that if your expectations match up with your experience, a good working harmony between you and the doctor will result.

Look around as you enter the office. Does it appear as though the doctor cares about the environment, and about you? Is the waiting room neat and inviting? Is the office assistant available or closed off in a glass cage that makes it impossible for you to talk freely?

A doctor's voice is best when it's level and controlled. Doctors who bark out questions—what's wrong with you today? what have you been doing to yourself? why are you here?—worsen your attitude. And the language doctors use to explain your problem is crucial. What's the point of using complicated scientific terminology that no one who hasn't studied medicine can understand, when simple English will always suffice? Why tell someone they're suffering from suppurative cholercystitis, when you can say that they've got a problem in their gallbladder?

These days, when most doctors finish their examinations, they walk out of the room without so much as a good-bye. I was taught to accompany the patient to the door and talk to them sympathetically. Doctors should also advise you when to return and warn you about any possible reactions to their treatments. You might feel as though a ten-ton truck had hit you for the next seventy-two hours, for instance, but there may well be no reason to worry, because after that period, the body will start to adjust.

If you're not happy with your doctor's attitude, think about finding someone new. You can't regain your health unless your mental outlook is good, and doctors that aren't helping could be hurting.

When should you see an osteopath instead of a medical doctor? Probably when you're not making any progress otherwise. Surely most people can tell when their own doctor no longer seems helpful. And an osteopath is useful anytime you want to maintain your health. You should have a checkup every year to make sure that your body remains in its proper alignment. These checkups are important. Survival in this society necessitates a highly functional body: as with an automobile, if the wheels aren't in balance, you can't drive straight down the street. The same thing is true of the human body: if it's out of its normal alignment, its chemistry won't function properly.

HOW TO BE A GOOD PATIENT

Trapped by endless rules and confused by indifferent medical programs, plenty of people feel alienated from their doctors. But even if you can't make your doctor more responsive, you can make yourself a better patient. Some of these suggestions may seem simple, but when it comes to taking care of yourself, details add up.

Before an appointment, always write down the reasons you're seeing the doctor and all the specifics of your ailment. If you've been feeling waves of pain, note the timing of those attacks, so the doctor can look for a pattern. If the pain has a daily schedule—worse in the morning, better at night—be ready to say so. If you've been taking medications, list them all. Too many patients freeze during their appointment, giving ambiguous answers, forgetting details, unproductively taking up the doctor's time. I can't tell you how often patients have come into my office and gone blank when I asked questions. Gee, Doctor, they ask, who could remember all that?

So many times I've treated a patient and given him or her a list of careful instructions, including a series of exercises, but the next time the patient came in, I would get a raft of excuses: oh, Doctor, I didn't have the time, I forgot to do them, I was too busy.

When all you've asked for is a simple five-minute exercise regime and the patient refuses to find the time to get it down, you have to wonder.

Some of my patients have actually said, Doctor, I just didn't want to do your exercises.

Early in my career, these excuses hurt me, because I was working as hard as possible, while the patient didn't seem to care. But after five or ten years I took the attitude that if the patient didn't heed my instructions, it wasn't going to worry me. That rationale probably helped me to survive my practice.

Another element to being a good patient is to endorse the philosophy of osteopathy, which holds that every body basically wants to be healthy. In osteopathy we consider structure and function as a unit: the bony structure must be in alignment for the rest of the body to function well, so if you have these two in balance, you're going to have good health.

Perhaps my patients don't believe this at first, but after the treatments, along with that feeling of wellness that follows, they start agreeing with me. They also tend to take their exercises more seriously and with a better attitude.

In fact, keeping a positive attitude toward yourself is always important. If you believe your doctor can't help you, you'll have a hard time recovering. The same holds true for your own thoughts. Develop faith in your recuperative powers, even if all you do is start to believe in yourself more. My experience has taught me that the better you think of yourself, the better your chances of being well.

You can help others' attitudes, too: when you heartily recommend a doctor to a friend, you are doing the friend a world of good, for you are starting the healing process right there with their excitement that someone can help them.

Listen to your body, which is in continuous communication with your mind. Some patients tell me that this sounds like silly mumbo jumbo, and then they'll describe their tension headaches or charley horses or stomach pains. This is the body's language. When you drink too much alcohol or exercise too much, the body's not going to speak up in English to urge you to behave. But it will talk to you through aches. Listen to them, and if they're telling you to keep off that ankle or lay off that food or stop taking that medicine, talk to your doctor about it.

Listen to your doctor, too. It's startling how many times I can tell a patient the same thing, yet over and over the patient refuses to listen. How hard can listening be? All you have to do is hear the words and let your brain digest them. So often I'll ask patients to demonstrate a breathing exercise they've just learned, and they get it wrong.

That's not how I instructed you, I tell them, but they shake their heads and swear it's what they heard. Now, maybe I'm so accustomed to giving the instructions that I talk too fast for the patient to comprehend. But since many do get it right, I couldn't be wrong all the time. Perhaps some people just have too many interesting thoughts going on in their heads to interrupt them, even for their doctor.

HERBS

Pharmaceutical drugs can be effective from the standpoint of treating the physical body. And that's it—that's all they can do. These drugs are chemical copies of single compounds—nature is much more complex—and don't have any life force in them, so they're only able to suppress a symptom. They can do nothing about the cause of the symptom.

Thus they can maintain your physical body, but they can't nourish it. The difference between the two functions is that while you're being maintained, you can be up on your feet, walking around and breathing, but you don't have enough energy in your body to do much else. When you're nourished, however, you can start living a full life again.

What drugs do best is enable the body to begin recuperating, getting back into rhythm. But in the long run, since most drugs address symptoms rather than causes, there are limits to their benefits. And since many drugs themselves cause other symptoms, people often end up taking four or five different ones at once. Let's say you go see a doctor for arthritis and he gives you a pain reliever, but along with that effect, the pain reliever also disturbs your digestive tract, so the doctor has to prescribe another drug for your stomach, and then that other drug may cause some other symptoms, and so you need another drug, and so on.

Herbal remedies, however, have that necessary subtle energy. They nourish the life field. They help the healing process begin, and when well prescribed, they don't have dangerous side effects. I know I couldn't have lived this long without using them.

I wish it were possible to tell you how specific herbs could help you, but they have to be prescribed individually for each person, just as any drug should be. In my case, because of my heart problem, I use hawthorn, which, just three days after I started taking it, began bringing some of the life force back into me.

The first step in taking herbs is to consult with a qualified herbalist. You can't just walk into a store, buy a bunch of herbs, and start ingesting them. You need to speak with someone who knows the field. Otherwise you may end up taking something useless or even harmful.

Each herb works for a different part of the body.

For instance, chamomile is said to cut inflammation in the digestive tract. Ginger may help nausea. Ginkgo biloba is used for blood circulation and is particularly beneficial for the elderly. Milk thistle seems to have good application for liver damage. Valerian, despite its unpleasant odor, may help certain people sleep. Frankly, I have a great deal of confidence in these herbs. Remember that modern drugs such as aspirin (from willow) and digitalis (from foxglove) originated as herbal remedies.

On the other hand, there is evidence that a few herbs now commonly sold in health-food stores may actually cause harm, such as comfrey and lobelia. This is why you must consult with a competent herbalist instead of simply buying items on the basis of the claims on their labels.

Today about twenty-five percent of all prescription drugs are derived from trees, shrubs, or herbs. According to the World Health Organization, of 119 plant-derived pharmaceutical medicines, almost three quarters are used in modern medicine in ways that correlate directly with their traditional uses as plant medicines by indigenous cultures.

HOMEOPATHY

Like herbal remedies, homeopathy adds nourishment to the life field. And you must be just as careful with homeopathy as you are with herbs. A great many people claim to know a great deal about both—but few have truly mastered these disciplines.

Homeopathy is based on the law of similars: a homeopathic preparation, a highly diluted formula, will produce in a patient a symptom complex similar to what the patient already has, and so the one displaces the other, and the patient becomes well.

The primary reason I'm so impressed with homeopathy is my very satisfactory association with a physician who taught at a nearby homeopathic college. He was determined to make a homeopath out of me, and so for many years he took every Thursday afternoon off from his practice to show me how he worked out his remedies. He also brought me along to visit many of his most interesting cases, and when I saw his remarkable results, I knew that homeopathy was worth studying.

What struck me most was the remarkable attention a homeopath gives to his patient. Before any formula is prescribed, a homeopath takes a lengthy case history. This series of questions and tests can last hours and will proceed through all the emotional and physical factors of the patient's symptoms until the homeopath feels confident enough to pick the best, and possibly the only, remedy.

I've had some real success myself with homeopathy, most recently with a child suffering from terrific spasms in his neck area. After talking to the

boy at length, I gave him the proper dose of a homeopathic remedy, and it proved remarkably effective. Twenty minutes later, he was calm enough
for me to apply my osteopathic manipulation.

At present homeopathy is generally ridiculed by
most medical doctors. And why shouldn't they ridicule it, when they're convinced that all they need
do is give you a pharmaceutical drug to suppress
your symptoms? But consider this: How many doctors have the time for homeopathy? One of the
country's best homeopaths used to devote at least
four hours a day to each patient, asking question
after question: where did the pain originate from?
what effect does it have? when is it strongest?

The drug companies also oppose homeopathy.
Since no one can patent nature's remedies, the in-
dustry can't make the necessary profits to make it
worth their while to market homeopathic formu-
las. So they do their best to prevent everyone else
from taking advantage of them, too.

The primary argument used against both homeopathy and herbal remedies is that no one can
prove their efficacy definitively. But many wonderful treatments in nature resist man's understanding. No one even knows why aspirin works, and
the fact is, if aspirin came along today, I'm sure it
would be banned.

When I started my practice, many excellent remedies were available, but since no scientific evidence existed to confirm they worked, they were
all eventually prohibited. And nature holds count-

less more potential cures that could do wonders for our health, but the scientific establishment continually blocks their realization, because no one can verify their capabilities. It's a shame modern science won't take the word of the hundreds of thousands of doctors and patients who have found these cures capable.

Many processes take place that science has yet to understand. Certainly no one can prove that consciousness exists: its nature is still one of science's greatest controversies. I don't see anyone saying we must ban it, however, because we can't confirm how it works or even if it's effective.

The art of medicine has never recovered from modern science's compulsion to prove in clinical laboratories that remedies work, even if they have already helped people. As a result, we have lost some of the best medications humanity has ever known. Don't ignore the healing potential of herbs and homeopathy just because your allopathic doctor discredits them. Over the years I've seen both work wonders in patients of all ages, suffering from all ailments. You simply have to be careful, and make sure you're consulting with someone who truly knows the secrets of these powerful remedies.

VITAMINS

I don't think anyone doubts that vitamins and minerals are essential for a healthy body. How we should get an adequate supply, however, creates more disagreement.

There was a time when Americans were able to obtain all their nutrients from their diet, which was filled with good meat and fresh vegetables and fruits. Supplements weren't necessary. But as the country's population increased and farming turned into a business, standards were lowered. A good deal of the food we now eat no longer has the life force needed to sustain our energy.

Therefore I do recommend that people take daily supplements, not only to guarantee that they receive adequate nourishment, but also this life force.

How many vitamins should you take? Which are best? When should you take them? The answers to all these questions, unfortunately, depend entirely on your individual system. But in general, I recommend that you try taking a multivitamin every day, instead of various separate vitamins and mineral tablets. Scientists don't yet understand which body needs which specific vitamins and in what proportions; it's probably impossible for you to intelligently prescribe for yourself only certain supplements. Equilibrium is the key, for then you'll have a more balanced chemical condition when the vitamins are breaking down in the body.

Most important, when you select a multivitamin, make sure it's completely natural. Synthetic vitamins don't contain the same vital life force as the vitamins derived from natural sources. This is another reason why we take supplements, to ensure that we're getting some of that life that we see in flowers and plants. Vitamins manufactured in the laboratories don't have this force.

The one specific supplement I myself take is brewer's yeast, which I sprinkle on my cereal every morning to guarantee that I'm getting all my B vitamins. Back when I had a practice, I used to work from eight in the morning until six at night, sometimes seeing as many as four patients in an hour while also making house calls, and often I'd skip lunch. In my particular case, the brewer's yeast helped me cope, because I knew that the vitamin B truly helped support my ability to touch and interpret that touch.

I also take a multivitamin tablet from a Naples, Florida, company called Health Center for Better Living Inc. And, ever since I developed that heart problem, I take a potassium pill, too, since potassium is one of the minerals absolutely necessary for the proper functioning of the heart and the brain.

Something else to remember is that your vitamin intake must be compatible. The vitamin C you take should work with the vitamin B and with the vitamin A, and so on. If the vitamins aren't making you feel better or if they're upsetting your digestive system, they're not working for you. Start taking those natural multiple vitamins, and see how you feel. When you find one that agrees with you, stay with it.

You must be your own guide. No doctor can

force you to swallow something you don't want. And no one can ever know you better than you can, although medical doctors might like you to believe that they do. The life force coming through your body is much smarter than their advice—if you can just listen to it.

Nutritional fads come and go, leaving in their wake all those who tried eating spirulina and protein powders and whatever else was fashionable for a moment. Some of these notions work, most don't. Still, I've always felt it was my duty as a doctor to investigate as many as possible. If a supplement was successful for me, I figured it might well work on my patients, and over the years I've tried innumerable vitamins, balms, and remedies, turning myself into both experimenter and guinea pig. For instance, not long ago a large consumption of cabbage juice was alleged to lower high blood pressure. So I went out and drank six ounces of the juice a day. Nothing happened. Then it was claimed that carrot juice would do wonders for your pressure, too, so I drank that; the juice gave my skin a nice brown cast, but little else.

I believe every doctor should experiment with change, and so my manipulative treatments have evolved over the years as I have learned new techniques. But these, too, I always tried on myself before patients. If the techniques were upsetting, they ended there; if they worked, I would apply them to others. During a few of these experiments, I've hurt myself. Once I tried a new treatment on my knee, and the next day it had swollen up so terribly that I had to turn to a friend for help. But I never hurt myself so badly that I couldn't recuperate.

Few fads are well founded. Too often they're just wishful thinking, or worse, someone's attempt to make money exploiting your health concerns. My recommendation is to leave the experimenting to people such as myself who have at least some background in evaluating the results.

EXERCISE

Vitamins aren't the only health aid that's beset by fads. In the last two decades some Americans have become so crazy about exercise that they don't realize how crazy they really are. People have taken a good idea and pushed it to such an extreme that some of them are hurting their bodies much more than helping them.

I see this happening in sport after sport. For example, quite a number of people currently lift free-weights or work out on machines until their bodies become as hard as bricks. Why do they do this? The body has a difficult time breathing when it's so tight. One Boston area osteopath I know used to keep a small sandbag in his office, and whenever overly muscled patients would come in, the doctor would hit them over the back with the sandbag to loosen up their bodies.

Worse problems occur if, after building yourself up for years, you suddenly stop.

The body always accustoms itself to a pattern of exercise. So when you stop cold, you're asking for trouble. Conventional wisdom says that the muscles turn to fat, but that's not so. Much more devastating results take place, because an abrupt halt can lead to a weakness in the nervous system, meaning that sometime in the future, when you need to pick up a heavy object, you won't be able to do it. In fact, if people who have lifted weights throughout their lives stop their routine suddenly, they may well end up in worse shape than those who've never touched a single weight.

The same is true for professional athletes, who spend far too much time repeating the same exercises, and then, once their career ends, stop altogether. Later in life they wonder why their health is faltering. Problems may not appear for as many as thirty years, but when they do, they can manifest themselves as a weakness in the cardiovascular system or perhaps as arthritis. Why? The constant repetitive exercise once kept all the blood vessels and the capillaries open, nourishing the athlete, but when the athlete stopped exercising, those capillaries started to clog, inflaming the bony structure. Such a condition may start off rather mildly, but when full blown, that's arthritis.

Remember, when the time comes to end a heavy exercise program, wean your body off of it carefully. Cut down on the number of days you're working out, the number of hours, and your general effort, until you're exercising one day per week, then twice a month, then once a month. Let your body gradually readjust to its new rhythms, instead of shocking it with sudden termination.

If you are forced to suddenly stop exercising, perform your exercises in your mind. This may sound strange, but I have found that by visualizing your routine, you are at least not breaking the mental pattern you have established, and this will be genuinely beneficial.

Aerobics can be a helpful exercise, stimulating the body's respiration. But aerobics can also be problematic if they aren't done in moderation. The trick to aerobics is to proceed at your own pace and ignore the instructor whenever you want. Many aerobics teachers don't have a clue what they're doing, because they're not doctors, nor are they really teachers.

The key words here are *attention* and *intention*. When you set out to accomplish something, you must first focus your attention on what you want to accomplish. After that, you have to keep your intention clear, to accomplish the thought pattern behind your actions. Presumably, you're performing aerobics to move your body and increase your heart rate, so you must pay attention to every step and every movement.

Most people don't. They get carried away with the music and the instructor's orders and they stretch their bodies further and further until, snap!—there goes the foot, and the ankle twists. They lost sight of their original intention, which was to improve their health.

I can't tell you how many people have come to me with injuries they've sustained doing aerobics. The oddest part is, once they've recovered, many of them go right back to their classes and hurt themselves again.

My experience has taught me that, of all the common exercises, stretching is the most helpful. If you stretch for ten minutes every day while paying attention to the rhythm of your breath and its movement through your body, you'll end up better toned and with a healthier exercise pattern—one that your nervous system can accept your whole life long—than if you took four classes of aerobics a week.

I've been doing the same basic exercises for fifty years. My personal favorite stretches are the following: I lie down on the floor and spread my feet apart, place my arms out to each side and slowly raise them out above my head along the floor, all the while feeling how flat my body has become. I do that for five to ten minutes a day. I also like to sit in a chair, bending forward at the waist, so my eyes look straight at the ground; then I hold my feet with my hands, and sit still for five minutes. This stretches out the lower portion of my back and helps to pull up the diaphragm, creating a deeper breath rhythm.

Another favorite exercise is to stand straight against a door, and with my arms extended from my body to the front parallel to the floor, I lift them as slowly as possible over my head.

While I stretch, I always monitor my breathing, listening to it closely and making sure that the breath coming out of my nostrils is equal on both sides. I also pay attention to my rib cage, sensing it work back and forth in a calm, easy motion. Sometimes I notice a little restriction in the inhalation phase, which means more stretching is required to loosen up wherever that restriction is located.

Let's say I find a problem on the left side of my neck: I'll sit in a chair and place my left hand on the chair's seat, or on a chair arm brace, while bringing my right arm up over my head and then pull the head toward the right, allowing all those muscles on the left side of the neck to stretch. After holding that position for a few minutes, I release it, reverse the hands, and continue until both sides feel balanced.

I don't stop until that good, prickly life force tickles my legs and feet.

Many doctors tell people of my age, or people fifty years younger, that walking is the perfect exercise. Walking can indeed be helpful for many people, but I've never had time to do much walking myself. But more important, there is no perfect exercise. Every one of us is an individual, and our bodies make different demands. The one thing we all need, though, is some kind of work for our breath and stretching.

Sometimes my patients tell me about some new study they've read that swears that everyone has to get a half an hour of vigorous exercise five times a week, or that we must all walk until we perspire, or that everyone's heart has to pump a certain number of times per minute. I dismiss it as one of the flaws in our educational system. So many people are struggling to get their PhD in order to find a job, and all of them are being forced to come up with a new theory and to publish one exhaustive paper after another. But rarely do they say much of worth.

The many doctors working in research institutions are also under constant pressure to write scientific papers and get their names in print. Yet after more than half a century of watching all these so-called groundbreaking studies come to light, I've noticed that sooner or later most of them contradict either what's been said before or what's said later.

Shun these fitness rules. The most important factor in finding the right exercise is whether you enjoy it. Otherwise you won't do it, or if you do, you'll hate it and eventually associate something as important as exercise with negative feelings.

There's nothing wrong with vigorous activity as long as it's right for you. But it often isn't. I know some people who've taken up running who don't ever want to stop, even when their knees start giving way.

Sometimes their doctors tell them not to worry: if it gets bad, they say, we'll just put in an artificial joint. But is that what you really want? An artificial joint? Although the artificial knees seem sound to me, artificial hip joints aren't. They produce wear and tear on the bony structure until it deteriorates, and pretty soon you're in as much pain as you were before that hip went in.

Don't worry about how much time exercise should take, either. Ten minutes a day of stretching has helped me reach ninety. The most important part of exercise isn't quantity, but regularity. Try to set a specific time for exercise every day, and do it consistently at that time. It's like always eating at a certain hour; the nervous system gets accustomed to it. And when you've developed a regular pattern, your healthy practice becomes automatic.

There is one form of exercise that can benefit a wide variety of people: yoga. Because it's meditative, yoga allows you to feel sensations in your body, such as the rearrangement or shifting of the muscles. And as you're observing these sensations, you can't help but also observe your breath and notice which part of the body is responding to the breath at that moment.

The only problem I see with yoga is that, like everything else in this country, people seem to want to do it better, do it harder, do it longer than anyone else. They end up stretching beyond the limit of their abilities, and soon they hurt themselves. Please, proceed at your body's pace, not that of your teacher's.

DIET

There are three factors that can most disturb the balance of the entire body: the barometric pressure, emotional tension, and diet.

When the barometric pressure falls, your blood sugar drops and your red-blood-cell count decreases, lowering the body's oxygen absorption. This can produce listlessness and aches. Conversely, a rising barometer causes a rise in the blood sugar, an increase in the red count, and an increase in the oxygen intake, all of which lead to vitality.

Emotional tension causes a contraction of the muscles below the head and a disturbance in the circulation to the brain, which stimulate abnormal nerve impulses, which in turn radiate throughout the body and create a general chemical distortion.

There's not much you can do about the barometric pressure, and emotional tension requires a good deal of work to remedy, but diet is something you can readily change.

How many people think about their diet? Do you actually stop to consider the food you're stuffing into your system and what the result of eating that food will be? Perhaps everyone wouldn't be shoving in so much food so quickly if they understood more about the body's reaction to it.

When a reaction does appear, however—in the form of indigestion, constipation, etc.—people simply soothe themselves by gulping down antacids or laxatives or whatever else they need to get their mistakes out of their body. Why doesn't it occur to them to stop eating the food that makes them sick in the first place?

The best statement that anyone has ever made about food is, eat a balanced diet. And yet people who write about food never really explain exactly what that means. In fact, all it takes is common sense. There has to be so much carbohydrate, so much protein, and a little fat in every meal.

The correct levels of each vary for each person and with activity level. There is no fixed percentage that every person should eat. Look at yourself, look at your body type, know yourself, and know your body. The better acquainted you are with your system, the easier it will be to figure out how much you should eat.

Let me give you a simple example of what it means to pay attention to your body's dietary needs. I can eat corn by itself, and I can eat lima beans. But when I eat corn and lima beans mixed together in succotash, I get the most splitting headaches you could imagine. So, although my body likes these two foods spearately, through the headaches it also says that something in the combination is wrong for me.

Most people's bodies react badly to at least some foods, but few people can identify them. Wouldn't it do you some good to know? Keep a food diary. Write down what you eat for breakfast, lunch, dinner, and snacks throughout the day. When you come down with a stomachache or a headache, see if you can spot a pattern. Pretty soon you, too, will be able to tell what foods don't agree with you. That's how I noticed that the succotash was hurting me. I realized I was coming down with severe headaches, and so I experimented, isolating different foods, eliminating and adding, until I located the problem.

Once you know more about your diet, act sensibly. So many patients come to see me with terrible indigestion problems and then tell me that chili, for instance, makes them feel bad, but they eat it anyway. What can I say to that?

Another dietary problem is haste. People dip into their food, take a huge forkful, and start to chew, but while their mouths are still full they're back at their plate for another forkful. Then they swallow before the food's been fully ground up and the digestive juices can break the food down and absorb the nutrients. These people are interfering with their digestive processes, and so they feel hungry, which makes them eat more food, and still more, until they've upset their systems.

Now, I've heard that some people recommend that you must chew food a hundred times before swallowing. Don't believe it. No one can set down a rule for everyone else to follow. Maybe my digestive juices work better than yours. Maybe my teeth grind up food more sharply. So maybe after fifty chews I'd be gnawing away at nothing, while someone else wouldn't have made a dent in the food. So why should we both swallow at a hundred?

There isn't a soul on earth who can tell you exactly how to chew, nor can they tell you the perfect diet unless they've studied you. So until that happens, be sensible, and eat what you enjoy, as long as you pay attention to your reactions. If you think chocolate is right for you, go out and eat a few bars, and then see how you feel afterward. You may start losing your equilibrium and even feel faint. Chocolate doesn't agree with most of us, but a small amount won't upset the whole metabolism, and each of us reacts to it differently.

The best way to conquer cravings for upsetting foods is to get more life force into your body and change your cells' patterns. Cravings are the sign of an emotional problem that wants to be satisfied by food. If the emotional pattern hasn't become too set in the nervous system, however, osteopathic treatment can break it up.

Another bothersome aspect of many modern dietary recommendations is that they pretend they're appropriate for you no matter how you use your body. If you're working outdoors in the cold weather, you'll need food that's going to produce a lot of heat, but if you're sitting at a desk all day,

you won't want a heavy meal. The diet books telling you to do it their way violate one of the world's
most basic laws, which is that people shouldn't try
to control others. You must control yourself,
through your own discipline, and not let anyone
else tell you what to do or eat.

Sometimes the problem isn't a given food as
much as what's in the food. Recently I had a visit
from a woman who was breaking out in hives and
rashes, and her dermatologist wasn't able to determine the cause.

I requested that she keep a chart of everything
she ate in the morning, at noontime, and evening,
and how she was feeling at the end of the day. She
did this for six weeks. Then, as we analyzed the
entire six-week picture, we found that on the days
she wasn't feeling well, she had eaten chicken pur-
chased from a local supermarket. So I asked her to
go out into the country and buy a chicken from a
farm and have it killed there.

When she ate that chicken, there was no response—no rash, not even a small outbreak. Then
I had her purchase a chicken at the store where
she originally shopped and cook and eat it. Afterward her body reacted again. Later investigation
showed that the company producing that brand of
chicken was spraying a great deal of antibiotics on
their birds to prevent spoilage. The woman was
highly vulnerable to the drugs, and her rash was
her symptom.

Despite my best attempts, some of my patients

don't pay the slightest attention to their diets. I've been treating one woman who keeps coming to see me because she's always got a pain in her lower back. I ask her about her eating patterns each time, and each time she claims that she's following the strict diet prescribed by her medical doctors. Then I ask her what she's been eating. I know it's responsible for her pain, but she won't believe me. She just giggles, as though I'd told a joke, and continues eating that harmful food. Meanwhile her medical doctors have informed her that she's developing osteoporosis equal to that usually seen in a seventy-year-old, yet she's only in her early fifties. Even that hasn't fazed her.

There's one food group you pretty much can't get too much of, and that's fruits and vegetables. They are among nature's greatest gifts to humankind. Not only do they taste satisfying and brim with nutrients that keep us vigorous and healthy, they contain a hearty helping of life force. The fruit of a plant has a higher frequency than the plant itself, just as the bloom of a flower is the full embodiment of that plant and has a higher frequency than the stem and the roots. Thus, foods such as apples and corn are the fruit, or the expression, of this vital force or subtle energy. Breath is one way we take in the life force, and these foods are another.

But unfortunately, given the manner in which our country's land has been mishandled and the pollution that's been absorbed into the ground, it's hard to get that good, healthy life force from food anymore.

Farmers ruin our land by overfertilizing instead of rotating crops and keeping the soil free from erosion. The crops keep growing, but the soil is never given an opportunity to rest. It's like gunning the motor of an automobile to push it through heavy traffic; the motor soon overheats. An overly fertilized plant is also overly stimulated and therefore doesn't absorb the full life force, because the ground doesn't have enough to give.

Corn is a good example of this unfortunate trend. We're growing stalks that are six to seven feet high, with ears much larger than ever, and the yield is huge. But each plant has less energy in it. (This is evident to anyone who feeds corn to animals, for it takes more corn than ever to do the job.)

That said, I must point out that I have found that vegetarians are among the hardest type of patient to treat. Their bodies just don't seem to have quite as much life force as those of nonvegetarians. This observation says less about the practice of vegetarianism than it does about today's vegetables. If the vegetables held vitality, people who ate nothing else would be fine. But since these vegetables are coming off land saturated in fertilizers, vegetarians aren't absorbing enough life force.

The same is true of processed and synthetic foods: there's no life force in them. I can't say that

I'm against them, because we have to eat something, but processed foods don't create much of a
healthy nutritional pattern within the body. That's
another reason why taking vitamins is so vital.

One other note on diet: Never underestimate the
role of water. You must be sure to drink an adequate amount every day, although again the
amount varies for each person. The formula I personally recommend is this: Take your age and di-
vide it by two. That's the minimum number of
ounces of water you need to drink daily. (This figure comes from a book by Carey A. Reams called
Choose Life or Death [Holistic Laboratories Inc.,
1990].)

Meanwhile, much of our drinking water has become contaminated, and rather than trying to
help, many politicians are turning their back on
this important issue. So drink the best water you
can find and afford, and pay attention to local reports about pollution showing up in your community water supply. If the authorities tell you to boil
it, then do so!

STRESS

Stress is what happens when your life force is
jammed.

Not that stress is always a bad thing. In some
ways it may actually be beneficial. An automobile
won't run well unless the tread on its tires is good

enough to grip the pavement. The same concept applies to the human body. Muscle has to be kept toned, and to a certain degree stress will assist in toning, so that when you're ready to get up and go, your muscles are ready to go with you.

Stress may even be good for the mind, keeping it in an active phase.

But unwanted stress can cause hardships. There you are at work, hunched over your desk, already feeling a great deal of pressure, when your boss comes over and tells you to get a little speed on.

What do you do? You draw in your breath and sit still for a moment, frozen. Truly, this might be one of the worst possible responses at a time when you most need your breath to flow.

If you end up carrying such stress within you, you upset the chemistry of your body, which can easily trigger a disease process.

Among the many patterns learned in childhood that remain imprinted in us for life is our manner of handling stress. Personalities develop around the age of three, at a time when we are approaching and touching everything in the house while our mothers and fathers are telling us not to. When we get a little older, we go to school, where teachers demand that we learn according to their rules only. We begin to play athletics and are judged harshly by our peers and coaches. All these situations create normal tension patterns, but no one teaches us how to handle them. Most of us respond by drawing in our breath and stopping the respiratory system from taking care of the stress, and this develops a negative pattern in the nervous system.

What's a better response to stress?

Take a deep breath in and out: when you take in air deeply, you are taking in all four types of breath. This relaxes the body enough to let the life force return, bringing you back into a state of well-being.

It also doesn't hurt to get up and go outside for a walk, which will engage all the muscles and spur them into action. Not running, but walking, which is much better for relieving stress. Once you get into the rhythm of walking, with your hands and feet moving together, the normal flow returns to your body and the breath gets into rhythm.

At home, when couples fight, the more quickly you both leave the tense environment and take a walk, the better you'll both feel. You'll start bringing action into your body, through the breathing and the movement. It's good to walk with each other, too, holding hands, letting that rhythm back into your bodies simultaneously.

MEDITATION

When people ask me if I know any other secrets to obtaining good health, I tell them I do: a quiet mind. A quiet mind leads to a more thorough understanding of your body, and with that understanding comes the knowledge of health.

Those still interested then ask how to help the mind become quiet. The answer to that is meditation. Not that prayer can't be useful, too, but prayer has a drawback: too many of us have been taught that prayer should be directed toward a God who exists outside of us, rather than within us. The advantage of meditation is that it can draw you inward, which is the state necessary to improve your health.

Because meditation silences the mind, it lets you become aware of your thought patterns. It gives you the chance to discover thoughts you've been hiding from yourself, ones you've never been able to express.

Thoughts and images that are unable to find outside expression can cause physical problems. Instead of leaving the body through words, they end up stuck inside the body itself. You already know that you never move a muscle without a thought telling you to do so. But these thoughts that don't get expressed also appear in the muscles, where they remain, because there's no movement allowing them to disappear. And there they cause trouble. For instance, the thought may cause the muscle to contract, and by doing so it will slow up your circulation as well as your nerve impulses, and that creates an area of congestion in which infection is likely to manifest. Anything from a stomach disorder to a stab in the chest area or tightness in the back of the neck can result.

While you meditate, a number of surprising concealed thoughts can surface in your mind. You might become aware that for years you've been carrying around images of someone who passed away, grief that you've been holding inside but never truly knew. And believe me, if your grief has never been expressed outwardly, it will be expressed inwardly.

Meditation can also help you become more radiant, because you're not burning up your vital force on a condition that's tearing you apart inside. And it helps you overcome the stress of today's chaotic environment.

Over the long run, meditation can also help you make progress toward spiritual evolvement, because by helping eliminate negative thought patterns, it will guide you toward a better appreciation of the world's magnificence.

There are many varieties of meditation. To discover which one works for you, simply sit and try out different methods. It's best to start without a guru or a mantra or a religion or a list of what's right or wrong. Just sit down, close your eyes, and try to stop thinking about your daily life and clear your mind.

I began meditating about forty years ago when the demands of my practice forced me to find some means of relaxation. Golf wasn't my answer, and so I read and talked to people until someone finally mentioned meditation, and then I taught myself how to do it.

In the beginning, I was happy if I could meditate for more than a few minutes. But eventually quieting the mind wasn't as impossible as it first seemed.

While I'm making my mind blank, I concentrate on letting the life force run through my body. I've been doing this so long now that it seems to automatically start the moment my eyes shut. I feel that tingling sensation, and often something snaps: perhaps some muscles fibers moved from a spastic state to release, allowing them to contract and relax; perhaps a bone shifted back to its normal position.

How often should you meditate, and for how long? The Good Book tells us to give one tenth of ourselves back to our creator. To me that means that not only should you donate one tenth of your earnings, but, since your body is your temple, you should give one tenth of yourself back to your own body. Therefore I meditate two and a half hours, which is about ten percent of the day. I usually start at half past three in the morning, and then I'm seldom aware of much until a few hours later, when my conscious mind returns.

After meditating this morning, I felt something break lose in the back of my neck, and when I rose, my body felt considerably more balanced.

Many people have told me that they've tried and tried, but they can't grasp the knack for meditation. Again, blame this scientific world that has taught us from the very first day of school to anticipate a tangible reaction to any action. When people sit down to meditate, even for the first time, they expect to be immediately proficient, and when they don't experience some quick sign of their skill, they fret, complain, and then eventually give up.

Meditation isn't about performance. It's about letting things flow. Not that things aren't always flowing—you wouldn't be alive otherwise—but most of us aren't aware of it. So meditation is also about learning to recognize and treasure the flow.

What's the best way to meditate? Find a quiet place where you won't be disturbed. It doesn't matter if you sit down, lie down, or stand up—whatever feels relaxed.

Wear something simple and comfortable that won't distract you and close your eyes, to block out the senses.

Stopping your thought processes takes discipline, but it isn't impossible. As thoughts appear, don't pay any attention to them. When you're first starting to meditate—and maybe for a long time afterward—you won't be able to keep hundreds of thoughts from popping into your mind. Don't hang on to them. Just listen to them, say hello, and then let them go. Another thought may appear right afterward. Repeat the procedure—acknowledge the thought's presence, and then let it go.

Don't worry if this process continues. For many people, it will happen countless times. Don't let that get you down. Be patient, and your patience will be rewarded.

If meditation still proves too difficult, here's one other tip: get down on all fours and crawl around the floor until your breathing becomes vigorous. This can make it easier to curtail your thinking, by putting you in an animal state and by helping your breath to flow with the universal force. You might want to be careful about where you try this out, however.

MORNING AND EVENING PEOPLE

Have you ever wondered why every morning your coworker arrives at the office wide-eyed and alert, while you're sluggish and tired, ready to roll back into bed? But at four o'clock, you're feeling energy flow into your body, while your coworker's eyes are barely open.

Most of us are either morning or evening people, and I suspect that the time you were born dictates this quality.

Just as the tide ebbs and flows, so does the world's energy. It begins to rise at about three to four in the morning, and it recedes twelve hours later. This morning energy influx helps explain why many people die at this time: their bodies are too weak to pick up the next day's energy. Without it their life force isn't recharged, and they pass on.

Your own personal energy cycle depends on your

birth time. If you were born while that energy was on the rise, you'll tend to become a morning person and function best before the energy drains away. But if you were born in the evening or the wee hours of the morning you will, for the most part, become a night person.

I have no proof of this outside of my observation that it almost always happens to be true among my patients, although the little research that's been done in this area is also convincing. Not long ago a shoe manufacturer commissioned a study to investigate how this knowledge might affect the workday. The researchers discovered that to get work done early in the morning, the manufacturer needed to hire people born in the morning, and for the late evening, hire individuals with night energy; by doing so the company realized a steady operational flow throughout the entire day.

What can an evening person do to work efficiently in the mornings? Or the morning person in the evening? Probably very little, although the effort is what keeps the coffee business so prosperous. The best you can do is maintain good respiration in your system, so it's always at a peak, and so are you.

As a morning person, I always tried to schedule my patients early in the day. I prefer having other morning people arrive first and evening people later, so that their energy levels were at their highest during the visit. Unfortunately, that proved too difficult to arrange, and so, because the evening people I saw at nine AM were often half asleep, their low energy pattern depleted me.

The discrepancy between morning and evening people can also wreak havoc on relationships. My best advice is not to force your partner to live out of synchronization. For instance, although I like to rise as early as three AM, I lived with a night person for fifty years. Just around the time when I was looking forward to a peaceful night's sleep, my wife would start cleaning out all the kitchen cupboards and vacuuming the floors. She eventually told me that if I would only cook my own breakfast, she'd take care of the rest of the meals. So I learned how to cook quite a good breakfast. There were plenty of hours left in the day to share.

At work, if you want the best results from your peers or employees, find out what time they were born. It won't do you or them much good to push them when they have little to give. The more you know about others' daily energy cycles, the better you'll get along with them.

JET LAG

Few people realize just how devitalizing an airplane trip can be to the human body. The reasons are myriad, including the lack of good ventilation, which upsets your respiratory system; the change in time zones, which throws off your internal time clock; and the harm done to the nervous system, which is knocked off kilter by your diet. Although you may be hungry at four o'clock, you have to wait another three hours to eat, and since you may end up three more hours from your original time zone, that's a six-hour wait, which can really tie your stomach in a knot.

As far as I'm concerned, just having to spend so much time sitting so close to other people's electromagnetic fields is upsetting. That's why I never sit in a middle seat if possible. Not to mention the other issues of an airplane trip, such as the discomfort, the noise, and, of course, the terrible food. Even the plane's vibrations are unhealthy. And, although you may not be aware of it, unconsciously you probably say to yourself every time you take off: I wonder if this plane's going to make it? That depresses the whole body's metabolism.

The entire environment of a plane these days is unfriendly. People talk loudly over the aisles, bump into each other, throw their seat back down into their neighbor's lap. The staff even demands that everyone lower the window curtains to darken the plane for the movie. Why should you pull the curtain down and deprive yourself of light while reading in order to accommodate a bad movie?

Depending on the flight's duration, one airplane trip can require a recuperation time of twenty-four to thirty-six hours. The best way to recover is to listen to the body and take care of it.

Last June, for example, I drove to Columbus, parked my car, and took a nonstop four-hour plane trip to Phoenix. When I arrived at the hotel, they announced that my room wouldn't be ready for still another hour, so I had to sit in the lobby amid all the confusion until they finally led me upstairs.

I then went to bed and stayed put until the next morning, when I got up at half past four and did my exercises; all this made me feel better. But if I had eaten and socialized, my whole body would have been thrown out of rhythm.

It's also important to take a relaxing bath. Not only does water help neutralize electromagnetic fields, it's comforting. (Bathing is often helpful to the spirit. We were all created in a water environment, and it's no accident that sinking back into a tub is soothing, as it reminds us of where we came from.)

If they don't compensate in some way for its ill effects, people in the habit of flying regularly from coast to coast don't have much of a chance of making it to ninety. They'll be lucky if their health holds up past sixty-five. When you look closely at their faces, you can already see the stress, the wear and tear.

THE SOLAR PLEXUS

Here's one of those ideas that leave many of the doctors who hear me lecture shaking their heads in wonder. They don't say anything aloud, but I know what they're thinking.

The solar plexus is a mass of nerve cells found in the center of the torso, lying beneath the heart and behind the stomach. From the solar plexus, nerves radiate out to all the abdominal organs. The solar plexus controls these organs, including the liver, pancreas, and kidneys, which is why a powerful punch to the solar plexus can knock someone out cold. This part the doctors accept.

However, I consider the solar plexus more than just a mass of nerves. I think it's something of an abdominal brain, where the emotions are centered, and from where they are generated. When people say that they have a gut feeling, they're literally correct—the feeling does come from the gut. And this is why so many people, when feeling overwhelmed by their emotions, suffer digestive problems.

The cerebral brain is more like a library and a computer. It holds all the memories and helps to bring out a person's desire and his will through the nervous system.

But the solar plexus also has the responsibility for maintaining and balancing the functions of the abdominal organs. Since nerve supplies circulate from here to the chest wall, the sex organs, the kidneys, and so on, when feelings such as anger, joy, sorrow, happiness, and hate are generated, the solar plexus must establish a balance among the organs and correct any organ dysfunction these emotions may trigger.

The normal newborn child has a greater abdominal than cerebral brain function. A baby can't talk, but it can take food and digest it, and if you stick a pin in the child, it feels the pain and cries. The cerebral brain doesn't begin to flourish until the child is almost three years old.

Listen to your gut. Too often people who say, I was offered a new job but my gut feeling is to turn it down, will take the job anyway, because they've been taught by modern society to follow their brain. Maybe they'd feel differently if they knew that the nerve endings in the solar plexus also constitute a brain, and sometimes these gut feelings are far closer to the truth than you would ever think.

Now, I didn't originate this idea; many other belief systems embrace similar conceptions of the solar plexus, and of the life force, too, such as Hinduism, with its conception of the chakras: the seven large energy centers in the human body. But the majority of Hindus live on a different continent, so western medicine doesn't take their opinions very seriously. In fact, most western doctors won't listen to any other kind of knowledge but their own. The thousands of years of wisdom accumulated by eastern philosophers doesn't mean much to them.

Why is it that so many people in this country fear the beliefs of others? It's as if western doctors' minds simply don't want to explore anything other than what they already know.

6

The Path of Life

Good health is more than a matter of taking care of your body. It means taking care of your head, your heart, and every other component of your life. No one lives apart. The more you pay attention to the ways of the world, the more likely your health is to reflect that attention in positive ways.

THE LAW OF GIVE AND REGIVE

The universe follows certain laws, and perhaps one of its most basic is a rhythmic balance interchange between opposite conditions.

More simply, it can be explained by three words: *give and regive*. In my case, I give my services to my patients, and they return to me their gratitude. Over the years I've received thousands of letters from former patients thanking me for my time and their good health. These people could have gone home and never said a word, but instead they took time from their busy lives to write, and their expression of appreciation repays me for what I've given to them.

Today, for the most part, the law of give and regive is sadly neglected. The contemporary version of the law would probably have to be restated as, how much can I get out of you, whether you like it or not?

Everyone wants more of what they're already getting. No one has the time, or cares enough, to give anything back. People expect to get more than their share or they feel they've somehow been cheated. Can you imagine a business deal where, instead of one side trying to take as much as possible from the other, the two sides reached a balanced equation and everyone walked away from the table feeling contented? Probably not.

Imagine if every time you did a favor, you received a note of appreciation in the mail.

Imagine if every time you remembered your friends with love, they remembered you, too.

Imagine if every time you gave of yourself to others, before long they helped someone else.

Because giving and regiving is a universal law, it has serious consequences. The other week a friend of mine and I drove to Missouri to present a lecture, and on the way we stopped at a roadside restaurant for some lunch. After the meal, while handing me my change, the cashier, noting my age and assuming I wasn't alert, shortchanged me by a dollar. Now, of course I noticed, but I didn't say a word, because my friend has a short temper and she would have exposed the man.

But over time that cashier will feel within himself sensations of guilt. He won't know where they're coming from, so he won't understand why they're present. He won't know what they mean, and he probably won't connect the feelings to his petty thievery. But those feelings will emerge nonetheless, and in the long run that man will pay more than the one dollar he took from me.

I don't believe that anyone can come away clean from that kind of act. We all have some kind of conscience, or we wouldn't be alive.

What you do for others will eventually return to you. Our emotional lives are connected to those of other people, whether we like it or not. You might want to believe that you're totally independent and that you can do and say whatever you wish. The truth is that we all share the same life force, and when you give or regive to someone else, you're helping your own life force grow.

It's not hard to spot those who never give to others. I used to see them all the time. These were the people who would stride into my office and object to almost any move I made. Well, Doc, they'd say, you didn't catch this pain last time, you didn't check my ankle to see if it was right, you didn't do a good job on me.

They're demanding, demanding, demanding. They can't relinquish their need to dominate others even when seeing a doctor. You can even discern it in their faces, in what appears as a darkened, depressed area on their cheeks, and in their eyes, where there's no sparkle.

Whenever I see a new patient, I study the face: the eyes and cheeks usually tell me much of what I need to know before the mouth ever opens.

People who fail to give and regive suffer because, as they age, they experience more aches and pains than they would have otherwise. Negative actions change the body chemistry. Essentially, you can't get away with doing the wrong thing. If you think you can, someday you may discover that your body is smarter than you are.

This law works through all of nature. For instance, when I was a young boy growing up on a farm, one of my daily chores was to milk the cows. Whenever I did, each cow would turn her head around and start licking my back. The cow was expressing the love that I gave her by relieving the pressure in her udder, by giving her food and water, and by providing her with a warm place in winter.

We often comment on how someone loves a pet, but it works the other way, too. A loving exchange takes place between pet and owner, and it's no accident that scientific research is beginning to show what anyone with any sense has always known: pets are good for your health. You give them love, they give you back love, and both of you are enriched by the process.

RELATIONSHIPS

Surely, the law of give and regive should be the basis for all our relationships. Unfortunately Americans don't know how to create good romantic relationships anymore. That ability has disappeared as certainly as horse-drawn carriages and manual typewriters. These days people choose a lover just as they might go to the fruit stand and pick up some grapes. As often as not, they end up at home with rotten fruit.

People are overly susceptible to infatuation. They don't look carefully. They don't think. They stop searching the first time they see something attractive. They're only looking at the surface, and they don't consider what's beneath.

A while back a former patient of mine told me that she was getting engaged to a fellow she'd just met. I wished her my best but added that I expected to see her again in about three months. She wasn't sure what I meant, although her expression indicated that she'd guessed. Well, the couple went ahead and married, and three months to the day that young woman was at my front door, wanting to come in and talk. You were right, she sobbed, things aren't a bit right with our marriage. Not long afterward, a divorce was in progress.

You must gauge people on more than appearance and momentary attraction if you want an enduring relationship. Here nature has given us a wonderful radiation that each one of us projects constantly, yet so few of us use it to sense our true partner. Haven't you ever stood next to people who seemed to emanate warmth, causing you to feel that something was special about them? It's as though they were surrounding you, inviting you into their very selves. It's the sensation of being welcome.

But instead of trying to appreciate this marvelous flow of the life force coursing through the body, most people's thought patterns are hooked on sexuality. Sex is not the key to a good relationship. A marriage won't work unless people abandon their fascination with a beautiful face and instead try to concentrate on a lovely soul.

In my entire life I've witnessed truly compatible relationships only a handful of times. Anybody can recognize one if they pay attention: look in her face, look in his face, and you can see that the two show a complete unity of spirit. I've seen this so rarely I can remember each individual incidence. Once, at an airport, I spotted a couple waiting to catch a plane, and I asked my wife if she didn't think that the two faces were the same. She looked at them and agreed that there was no difference in the expression coming from their life force. Very few people are matched so well. But any couple who allows their mutual attraction to stem from the life force, rather than from superficial appeal, can succeed.

MARRIAGE

The priorities in a marriage aren't complicated. First comes the spouse, then the child, and, finally, the job. In a good marriage, the couple works together to help each other achieve their goals. And when the two of you function in the above order, things are most likely to run smoothly.

But if you allow your work to become the dominant area of your life, you're demoting your spouse to a second-rate position, and soon your spouse's negative feelings will trickle into the relationship. Before you know it, you're no longer compatible.

If it's the male who ignores the female, often she will turn a child into a husband-replacement, which can destroy the marriage. (Until recently this sort of mother-child bond occurred fairly frequently, but the recent admission of fathers into the delivery room has lessened the risk. Whereas once all the father could do was pace and worry while the mother forgot she had a partner waiting outside, the father can now become closely involved in childbirth, establishing the correct pattern for a lifetime father-child relationship.)

One of the next most important commitments

you can make to your spouse is to maintain your health. I have one patient who, during her menopause, has become unusually irrational and unpleasant, infuriating her husband, driving the relationship to the brink. All she needs is a few good doses of calcium to balance her chemistry, but she won't find the time to take it.

And I know plenty of men who, rather than attend to their blood pressure, allow it to rise to the point where they vent their anger on those who are around them. Unfortunately, it's most often their wives.

Another factor to consider in marriage is diet. We understand which foods are best for us by paying attention to our systems and trusting the body's messages. Yet couples sometimes forget this because they in essence shop for two. Maybe the food they eat is compatible for one of them, but not for both. Digestive systems are as different as personalities. If you've identified the foods that work for you, make sure the rest of your family does the same. You can't instill your dietary preferences in someone else, no matter how much you love them or they love you.

CHILDREN

A relationship with a child doesn't begin the moment the child is born. It precedes birth.

Even while the child is in the womb, an intimate, two-way communication is taking place between the fetus and the mother. This represents more than an internal chemical relationship. The mother's life field carries specific information about her emotional state and her experiences with the pregnancy. In the book *The Secret Life of the Unborn Child* (Summit Books, 1983), authors Thomas Verny, MD, and John Kelly offer impressive evidence of this communication. They also stress the value of the father's presence during the mother's pregnancy, as well as the importance of the mother's emotional calmness and happiness in the process of bonding.

Both parents should be encouraged to talk to their unborn child about the love and joy created by the thought of the upcoming birth. The baby can't comprehend the words, but the ideas nonetheless seem to be communicated.

Once the child is born, my experience says, the most important years of its life are the first three, and if there's any time that diet is crucial, it's now.

Most of all, the child shouldn't be fed on an erratic schedule. The parent must provide a consistent pattern to the diet, so that, as the child ages, that pattern remains intact. In the long run, this will optimize the child's general health.

The body gets accustomed to the routines of food, both the type and the timing, and customary feeding establishes a pattern that helps guarantee better health. The chemistry of the nervous system always does best when given a routine. The people who grab a quick cup of coffee and a sandwich at odd times during the day are asking for trouble later in life.

To my mind the nervous system is something like a computer software program for the body. On a computer you type certain keys and you get certain results; in the body, you commit certain actions and the nervous system kicks in.

Adults should watch dietary patterns in their children as closely as they do in themselves. Children who eat a certain food and spit it out a few minutes later may well be telling you something important. A child doesn't have any other way of saying something is detestable.

One disturbing pattern I've noted among many of my young patients is that they don't get enough exercise. The parents place the kids in the playpen and keep them there as long as possible. They say that otherwise that child will crawl all over the furniture and destroy it. Well, that behavior may not be good for the sofa, but it's good for the baby, allowing it to stimulate activity in the muscular system and help develop the brain cells. You can always buy a new couch.

One caveat: Don't get your child walking too early. Too many parents are trying to persuade their children to start earlier than the normal eleven or twelve months, and so they balance them on chairs and stand them up on tables to get them going. Don't do this. Children need to go through the developmental stage of crawling. I've noticed that children whose parents forced them to walk too quickly (what a precocious baby, the parents exclaim) may even suffer learning difficulties in school. The human body is designed to develop in certain ways. It's not just a matter of waiting for legs to become strong enough to support the child; the nervous system must advance properly through each developmental stage.

I can give you an example from a family on whom I've done a good deal of work. Of the four children, the first didn't walk until he was about fourteen months old, which is a little older than normal. He turned out to be an excellent student. His two younger siblings were walking by the time they were eleven months old, and they were average students. By the time the youngest baby came along, all his siblings wanted him to start walking early. With that kind of encouragement, he was up on his feet at eight months, and he ended up a slow learner.

One last thing. When children fall and hurt themselves, let them scream. The crying will get their breathing process stabilized and maximized. If the diaphragm can get into motion within five to ten minutes, there's nothing to worry about. Otherwise the body might well lock that trauma inside. So it's fine to comfort your children, but don't stand in the way of their breathing, or you're doing no one a favor.

EDUCATION

In the last decade prominent women and men from numerous fields have been looking into such matters as the long history of unexplained recoveries among terminally ill and injured patients; the role of imagery, affirmation, and prayer in stimulating the body's healing response; the power of such techniques as biofeedback and meditation to provide people greater control over their bodies; and the unusual dreams of scientific giants, including Albert Einstein, some of which produced history-making breakthroughs.

But are our children being properly educated to continue the work in these areas?

My sense is that they're not. Our current education system is faulty. Today's schools teach performance. They demand children memorize and absorb rather than learn. Teachers know one way to teach, and one way only, and students must learn that way, mostly to please the teachers. Tomorrow's lesson will be the next ten pages, they say, and you'd better read those pages and be prepared to recite them back in a way that will satisfy us.

I see this even in my practice, when I try to help young children learn to breathe. Rather than trying to understand, they prefer showing off how well they can perform. I'm not interested in performance. I'm interested in the movements themselves and the activity they'll create within the body.

Our current education system fails to help individuals develop their creativity. Nor does it foster a sense of wisdom. It only helps students get the grades they need to advance to the next level.

Yet we know that many of the best scientific minds of our century came to their ideas not through stale performance, but through creativity. Einstein, a truly spiritual physicist, was perhaps the greatest. His own words speak with great eloquence of the prime motive for his life and work: "I want to know how God created this world," he said. "I am not interested in this or that phenomenon, in the spectrum of this or that element. I want to know His thought, the rest is detail."

Most scientists lack the spirit of adventure that permitted Einstein to ride on a beam of light to the farthest reaches of the universe while sitting in his backyard, scribbling the secrets of the cosmos on the back of an old envelope.

No one ever asked Einstein to prove his theories. He never did any experiments; he never had a laboratory. All his work was proved by others who had the skill to perform such tasks.

Einstein realized that despite his famous name and a creative power second to none, the world would not only abuse his knowledge, but ridicule his more serious ideas while praising his more limited concepts. In fact, it is hard to find scientists who have read all of Einstein's more esoteric works. It takes a seer of the same order as Einstein to penetrate the various dimensions of the energies of consciousness and present a theory as workable as $E = mc^2$.

Another of these scientific giants was Nikola Tesla, the spiritual inventor. Tesla is hardly a household name, yet if it weren't for his discoveries, today's typical household would look quite different. It was Tesla's invention of the first practical alternating-current dynamo and transmission system that made the electric age possible.

Tesla's unusual powers of visualization first appeared in his early years in the form of an affliction. The young Tesla was tormented by terrifying memories of such clarity that he felt he was witnessing two realities: the world around him, and the detailed re-creation of a world from his past.

To free himself from these phantasms, Tesla decided to refine them into a tool for dreaming up his inventions. He didn't need to make models or drawings or perform experiments; all he had to do was set his mind's eye to work. He began to evolve what he later considered a much more efficient approach to materializing inventions than the age-old process of trial and error, sketch and experiment.

One day he was challenged to build a more efficient dynamo. The solution came unexpectedly, while he and a friend were walking through a park, reciting poetry. He later wrote: "As I uttered these inspiring words, the idea came like a flash of lightning, and in an instant the truth was revealed. I drew with a stick on the sand the diagrams shown six years later in my address before the American Institute of Electrical Engineers, and my companion understood them perfectly. The images I saw were wonderfully sharp and clear and had the solidity of metal and stones, so much so that I told him, 'See my motor here, watch me reverse it.' A thousand secrets of nature, which I might have stumbled upon accidentally, I would have given for that one which I wrested from nature against all odds and at the peril of my existence."

Creative solutions, generated in the out-of-conscious-awareness processes of the mind, often stream into awareness in the form of images to be materialized.

If I ran the schools today, my first act would be to rid them of their pattern of dominating children and instead encourage this kind of dreaming and creativity.

Why don't teachers try to engage students' interest in a similar manner? Why don't they create problems for them to solve and allow each one to solve them individually, in their own way, letting the students develop their full creativity and open-mindedness? The Einsteins and Teslas of this world are notorious for doing poorly in school, but doing well in life.

Basically, the conventional American school system was formulated to produce workers for a growing economy. It teaches us how to perform so we can pursue our material desires, whether those desires are for a car, a television, a sound system, or any other gadget we use for a short while and then discard. By the time we're through school, we're ready to absorb every aspect of this country's economic production.

But is this kind of instruction really best for us? Wouldn't it be valuable to develop more than our ability to perform? What about our wonderful ability to make inner contact with the universal forces that first created us? Learning isn't just a matter of striving for the best grades or the best possessions. It's also about striving to know our spiritual side, for in this place reside the answers to more questions than any teacher ever asked.

The best remedy for having gone through this kind of education system is to take it upon yourself to read. You don't need a school for learning. Ask people you respect for recommendations, read at your own pace, and interpret the thoughts. Try to conceive your own understanding of the book's meaning, rather than the one that you imagine is correct. You'll learn what someone else has to say, and you'll learn more about yourself in the process. And always take notes. When you've finished, go back over these notes and you can feel the stimulating effect of the thoughts recorded.

DEATH (AND AFTER DEATH)

I believe that birth isn't the beginning of life, but the beginning of death.

Look at your cells. At various intervals each of them dies and is replaced by a new one. So, in a way, you're continually living in a new body. We're all dying constantly as life is constantly being replaced. But as you grow older, Mother Nature loses her capacity to replace those cells as fast as they deteriorate. One day the process can't go any further, and that's death, as far as the material world is concerned.

I often think of death as being the final exchange. What are we exchanging? Life in this world for some kind of life in another.

I do believe in an afterlife, but I can't conceive of it. No one can. You can read all kinds of books, you can talk to all sorts of people, but my hunch is that we're not supposed to know the answer, and we never will.

Dr. Burr, monitoring trees with his voltmeters, found that the life force drained from a tree as it died and guessed that the force must have departed for elsewhere. And scientists have recorded on film a sudden electrical pattern at the moment of human death, although no one yet knows what that pattern represents. I'd like to think it means that something leaves the body for an uncharted voyage to an unknown destination.

Each of us on earth has a personality, but that stays behind. The personality is only a creation of the material world. We all have a life force, too, and although that life force comes from the same source, it's slightly different in each of us, and that's what makes us unique individuals. Just as there are no two identical DNA patterns, there are no two identical life-force patterns.

After we die, unlike the personality, the life force continues to exist and then returns to earth in some other form. What that form is, I don't know.

Because of my beliefs, I'm not afraid of death. Many other people are, however, and I suspect their fear is generated in part by a lifetime of negative emotions, as well as a lack of commitment to society. When the time of death arrives—and it will come to all of us—sit back and review your thoughts and actions: if you haven't led an existence filled with love, you will realize how empty your life has been. You will become afraid. You won't want to die, because you realize that you have never truly lived.

I've observed many people pass away. Some die gracefully, while others go through soul-searching torment. One group is secure; the other is afraid of the unknown possibilities that may have to be faced.

EUTHANASIA

Sometimes it seems the fear of death is systemic.

Medical science certainly doesn't seem willing to let us die anymore. Someone told me recently that it won't be long until Americans will routinely live past 110. It's amazing, he said, what technology can do. Isn't it great?

I don't think it's so great. I think it's a problem. What kind of lives will we be living? For many, they will be filled with inertia and emptiness, sitting listlessly in a home or hospital, incapable of giving anything back to society. What is the sense of forcing someone to remain alive for so long?

Yet we don't seem to know how to stop. We don't even want to consider the consequences. A friend of mine recently discovered that his eighty-seven-year-old father had developed serious heart trouble and wouldn't be able to live without a pacemaker. My friend spent weeks trying to make up his mind whether or not to buy the machine, but finally he felt he had to. The father lived, but his mental attitude changed, for the shock of the operation nearly destroyed him, and now he's basically inert.

Once people reach a certain time in life, it's better to let them peaceably pass on. That time varies for each individual: some people are active, vibrant members of society past the age of one hundred. But today we're extending the life of too many who can no longer handle its responsibility.

Death is the end of the physical, material body. But the life force passes on. Each patient should be allowed to pass on, too.

7

The Human Spirit

Much is said these days about spirituality, but it still remains a vague mystery to many. Here's how I've advised patients to understand their spirit in order to help heal their body and mind, as all three—body, mind, and spirit—must be in balance for an individual to flourish.

THE TRIUNE HUMAN

"Man is triune when complete. First, the material body; second, the spiritual being; third, a being of mind which is far superior to all vital motions and material forms. . . . Thus to obtain good results, we must blend ourselves with, and travel in harmony, with nature's truths."

—ANDREW TAYLOR STILL

The philosophy of osteopathy, as proposed by Dr. Still, presumes that every person has three bodies. One is spiritual, another is mental, and the third is material.

Dr. Still didn't elaborate enough on this concept to satisfy me, so much of my life has become a search for more information. My synthesis to date (for such a quest never ends) combines my knowledge of osteopathy with eastern thought and, in particular, Taoism.

Spirituality means the ability to find peace and happiness in an imperfect world.

It also means understanding that one's own personality is imperfect, but acceptable. From this peaceful state of mind comes both creativity and the ability to live unselfishly.

This spiritual part of the body can't be seen or heard, or felt by the senses, but it can be known. That which can't be seen, but which can be known, consists of such qualities as faith, forgiveness, peace, love, beauty, happiness, joy, and ecstasy.

The spiritual body is composed of three parts: our consciousness, our intuition, and our communication.

Consciousness is that substance that allows us to survive; it tells us what's good and bad in life. You'd be in a coma if you weren't receiving some of this energy of the spirit.

Intuition is the psychic part of our mind, the direct access to the spiritual side, which, unfortunately, very few of us experience, as intuitive notions are like precious jewels of thought, and are rare.

Most of us, however, feel minor levels of intuition. For example, after being introduced to a stranger, you may walk away feeling that the person's voice had a note of sincerity. The *sound* of that voice is part of the created universe that the senses feel, but the *sincerity* is a part of the silent universe that can only be known through intuition.

Communication takes place between you and your spirit. Although many people's actions don't allow their spirituality to seep into their thought patterns, every man, woman, and child on earth has access to the spiritual aspect.

The spiritual nature leads us toward an integration with the forces behind creation, which is a loving, intelligent energy.

I have never seen any proof that spirituality is connected to organized religion. Spirituality is chiefly concerned with raising individual consciousness—which will make a person more considerate, more kind, and more loving—and not with joining an organized society.

I am certainly aware that modern science rejects the idea of spirituality. But it is possible to be both modern and spiritual. In fact, a rebirth in spirituality is taking place right now, as scientists are testing and validating human energy transformations. Perhaps we are on our way to the glorious revelation predicted by the French Jesuit philosopher Pierre Teilhard de Chardin: "Some say, after we have mastered the wind, the waves, the tides, and gravity, we shall harness for God the energies of love. Then for the second time in the history of the world, man will have discovered fire."

There is the mental body, too, which contains the mind, whose duty it is to manage wisely this great engine of life.

The mind and the body communicate continuously with each other, but most of this communication occurs at an unconscious level. The mind is the force that allows the body to accomplish.

The mind exists in space around the body. It isn't the brain, but rather a formative force of the brain.

In the mental body there exists the desire and the will.

Desire can be overwhelming and is usually oriented toward the material—the desire for a new house, for a fancy car, for more money. These days too many people choose to follow their basest desires, madly rushing to accumulate all the material possessions they can find.

Have you ever walked through a town and seen people who look forlorn, not because they lack money, but because they are devoid of spirit, despite all their possessions? They're the product of their desires, and they look it—empty, hardened, spiritless.

Desire is kept in check by means of the will. Using the will to be the finest person possible is the best path to becoming purely spiritual.

Occasionally I've been able to convince patients of this relationship between desire and will and have even persuaded some to change their behavior for the good of their health. For instance, many years ago a man came to me after being discharged from the army due to a hyperactive emotional response as well as physical nervousness, from which his doctors had told him he would never recover. I then described to him the concept of desire and the will, and I let him know that the army doctors had put the notion in his head that he was ill, and as a result he had developed the desire to remain so.

But you still have the life force within you, I said, and so you've got the will to overcome that desire. I then gave him several manipulative treatments along with a series of breathing exercises to rid him of that emotional pattern. The man chose to follow his will, and his jitters have never reoccurred.

There is also a material body, or the actual body, an instrument through which you express yourself. Medical science has identified the primary systems of this body: the circulatory system, digestive system, autonomic nervous system, and the immune system.

Dr. Still called this material body of man the

Great Machine. The machine has a heart, which is the engine; the lungs, which are a fan and a sieve; and a brain, which, with its two lobes, is an electric battery. The material body as a whole has a wonderful chemical laboratory inside that only the mind could conceive.

This machine is run by the unseen forces called life. It is self-creative, self-developing, self-adjusting, self-repairing, self-recuperating, self-sustaining, and self-propelling.

Like all other things, the material body is composed of electric waves of light, the same waves that illuminate our houses or bring us television, and it is held together by a complex network of electrical and electromagnetic energy fields, which I have already called the life field.

The material body brings with it the powers of reasoning and instinct. If will is controlled by animal instinct, we are lead to desires. If it is controlled by reasoning, then we are lead to the spiritual.

FINDING THE SPIRIT

Every human on this earth, regardless of age, race, or nationality, is a completely pure being, because each and every one of us receives our energy from the same universal source.

Goodness is the ability to maintain a close connection to this pure, spiritual nature, which is always present and always accessible to every one of us.

Evil, on the other hand, doesn't exist. But evil can happen, nonetheless. People become evil when they block off that purity, that life-giving universal flow of energy, from their being. Thus, evil represents the absence of the spiritual force. Adolf Hitler became evil when he severed his connection to his universal purity and instead chose to become controlled by his mind's desires. Purity was always present in his being—it's there in all of us, by universal design—but he had blocked the communication between his heart and his mind.

The failure to connect to nature's pure side happens far too often today, throughout practically every segment of society. You can observe it in corporations, in personal relationships, in politics, in religion, in the media. You can find it in cities, in suburbs, and in rural areas.

Writer and philosopher Walter Russell created a metaphorical image that can help us understand our times. Draw a line on a sheet of paper and find its center, which represents the neutral point of our lives. On one side of that center is the positive energy, or the spiritual side of life; on the other side is the negative. Everything depends on where a pendulum suspended over the line is in relationship to that neutral point. For most of us it swings back and forth, never coming to rest in one place. You've had occasions, as have I, when you wanted to slap someone down in anger or envy or to speak out in rage. For the most part we restrain those feelings, and we're able to swing far enough to the positive side to balance whatever thoughts are emerging on the negative.

This metaphor applies to us as a species, as well. Since the early part of this century the pendulum has been drifting toward the unfavorable side. But I'm quite optimistic that it's currently moving in the other direction and that we will soon be witnessing social changes that will shepherd us to a better society in the next decade.

If you look closely, you can see some of these shifts already appearing. For instance, this past Sunday one of the retired ministers in our community conducted a beautiful service, spending a good deal of the time talking about his gay son, whom he loves very much. I would wager that five years ago he would never have ventured forth on that subject. I've also witnessed signs of change on television, most recently when a young actor presented his plan for adapting the Bible to a video format for young children to watch at home. His producers wouldn't underwrite the project, so the man is doing it entirely out of his own funds. In fact, it's in the burgeoning area of child care that I see the most hope, for when a country is concerned with the welfare of its children, it will produce a more respectful generation to come. The future of our children is joined to the future of society, because they're the ones who will construct that society.

Of course, the surest way to guarantee that these changes will occur is for every one of us to get in touch with the spiritual part of our nature.

There are numerous ways to find that spiritual side. But first, you need to develop a sense of your life's ultimate purpose.

And what is that purpose?

That I can't answer—finding it is part of your lifetime's work. I would guess my own purpose has been to develop my skills as a healer and an osteopath; perhaps that's why I was turned down by medical school, to help me get on the right track.

How important is it for you to figure out your purpose? I don't know of anything more important. To feel genuine satisfaction at your life's end, you must try to leave something behind that has been truly beneficial for the general welfare of humankind. This is what your purpose accomplishes for you.

I wish we trained our young to understand this. We encourage them to live a joyful, happy life, but we omit that so much of the world's joy and happiness derives not from how much money we accumulate, but from how much we give to the world for the benefit of others.

And what if you don't achieve your purpose—or you don't even try to achieve it? If you wish to witness what happens to those who are purposeless in life, be present at the moment of their death. As I've said, I've had many opportunities to watch such people pass away. Their death is a battle; they seem to be grasping, as though something were missing from their souls. They seem to be thinking, I'd be all right if I only had something to hold on to.

Compare that struggle to the death of those individuals who've made their lives worthwhile. They close their eyes peacefully, they let death in, and then everything shuts down. The serene expressions on their faces tell me all.

Many people complain that they want a sense of purpose but that nothing in their life has prepared them properly for finding one. It's never too late to try, and there's plenty of information available. I myself have been so lucky that, whenever I needed to learn about something new, someone sent it to me. But perhaps that's not so unusual. People are so preoccupied with this material world that they don't realize that the world is awash in wisdom if they would only open their eyes wide enough to see.

What are other avenues to the spiritual side?

Help a stranger to cross the street, or offer someone needy your seat on a bus. Whenever you're willing to give to others without strings, you inspire a small burst of life. The other person begins thinking about giving back, and the law of give and regive is sparked.

Go outdoors and touch a tree or sit and observe the beauty of a flowering plant. That was how I was taught by Marcel Vogel, my engineer friend at IBM. He told me to select one particular tree and to put my arms around it every day until I could sense the radiation coming into my hands. And that's what I did, and eventually I was able to feel that force.

I've always told my patients to go out and do the same. They may suspect I'm odd, but they finally realize that all I'm really asking them to do is associate with Mother Nature. I wouldn't be surprised if by the time I had left Cincinnati, every tree in that city had a human companion.

Have you ever seen pictures of the Chinese standing in parks or streets, waving their arms while doing their *tai chi* exercises? There's little difference between hugging a tree and doing those exercises. Both lead you to the spirit.

For those who live in urban areas where greenery isn't abundant, I urge you to buy a plant and adopt it. Water it, nourish it, and place it in the glow of the light from your window. That plant will give back to you energy that will radiate throughout your apartment. If you don't believe me, move the plant somewhere else for a few days and you'll feel a shift within yourself—a piece of life is missing from your room.

Give and regive. Why? Because every time you do so, you're radiating the same life force that exists in every tree, every flower, as well as in you. We forget sometimes that man is just as much a part of nature as plants and animals, but his desires, as experienced through his senses, make him feel separate.

Another wonderful path to the spiritual side is a visit to an art museum, where you can appreciate the tremendous life force of the artists who brought those unique paintings into existence. Such experiences help stimulate your own life force. Sitting in a quiet gallery can also help you reach a state of meditative contentment. Yet on any given autumn weekend in America, many art museums stand almost deserted, while hundreds of thousands of people sit in football stadiums, bellowing and screaming as twenty two men destroy one another's bodies.

Please, sit down soon and consider your life. Reflect on the actions you've taken to further your spiritual side. Make a list of them on a piece of paper, to make sure you're giving this area of your life the proper attention. Also, think about where you have been misdirecting your energy and where have you been using it wisely.

Enjoying nature or doing a favor for someone else with no expectations or taking pleasure from the fruits of someone else's creativity—all these help unlock blockages. This loosening of the life force strengthens your health, because the more contact you have with your spiritual side, the more your energy flows freely through your body.

LOVE

Love is the energy that expresses the spiritual force.

The more you sense that force coming through your body, the more love you can feel.

When you are able to love without constraint, you maintain a balance of forces that keeps your body, mind, and spirit functioning and moving in a direction of growth.

The art of loving is the ability to recognize and respect in each person the essence within. Once you recognize the beauty of that essence, you become drawn to the person. That person is likewise drawn to you. No longer are there two persons, but one, created in the love that you share with each other. The act of loving is to make another person whole. Love is about giving, and regiving.

LOVE AND HEALING

The act of healing through touch brings a person into a state of wholeness, helping that person to connect with his or her essence.

The laying on of a healer's hands assists in linking a person's essence to their body, so that the life energy can start to flow fully again.

Through the use of the hands, a healer then balances the force in the body.

Through the will, a healer projects love to the patient. And the patient, relaxed in the presence of a caring healer, accepts that love.

Love should be part of every doctor's practice, because a patient can sense that love. Whenever a doctor walks into a room where a patient is waiting, that patient should immediately feel good. The patient should think, here comes help.

Patients recognize love. A few days ago I treated a young girl who refused to crawl; she had no energy, no vigor. So I loosened up her body and got her breathing well again. This morning her mother was nice enough to call and tell me that when they arrived home, her daughter immediately began crawling around the floor vigorously. The mother told me how elated both she and her husband were. The effects of what I projected into the child were projected in turn by the child to the parents.

Healing, too, is about giving and regiving.

EVOLVEMENT

Up to this point I've discussed maintaining physical, spiritual, and emotional health. There is a step beyond as well: evolvement.

A person's evolvement is based on the development of his or her will. Remember, the mind possesses both desire and will. Everyone must ask, What am I going to put my willpower behind?

I believe that the human race is continuing to evolve, and that this evolvement will manifest itself in our DNA, in our hormones, and throughout the entire human body.

Earlier I spoke of a wrong turn this country has taken, away from the spirit and toward an obsession with materialism and selfishness. I suspect this arose from this century's many tragedies. World War II, for example, disturbed and damaged the national mood. With large numbers of men gone, too many children were brought up without a father, and everyone became accustomed to a life of sacrifices. Then there followed the Korean War and the Vietnam War, each more problematic than the last. The trauma of wars, and of one immense social change after another, leaves a country bereft, causing the pendulum to swing away from noble impulses, creating an atmosphere of material desires and a disrespect for spirituality.

But today I see signs of hope for humanity at large, as an increasing number of individuals are becoming interested in evolvement. There are many ways to initiate this process. Certainly becoming more spiritual is the first step. You can also spend more time understanding the invisible inner world. It's in this world that you must make changes. You must uncover, and transform, your thought patterns. Here's where so many land in trouble: they don't want to think about their past actions or past experiences. They've been schooled to believe that life is about the present, and the future, and that success depends upon focusing on what you're doing now and what you will be doing. They seldom stop to think that the activities of the past may well have created their present problems and will continue to produce future ones.

Few people understand that trauma, physical or psychological, imprints itself in the nervous system. But when you can rid yourself of the effects of negative past experiences, the body chemistry changes and you become more open to evolvement. Your attitude toward the world changes, and you start to feel a glow, the radiation that emanates from the higher frequencies resounding in the body.

What does a sense of greater evolvement feel like?

For one, you will walk around feeling as though you were on springs, because you will be absorbing the energy of nature's beauty. Where most people live in a state of inattention, you'll be invariably struck by the loveliness around you, and that connection will be strong and enriching.

You will also manifest evolvement by the manner in which you express yourself. You will communicate your inner health to the rest of the world. You will always be willing to help other people. Regardless of the demand, you will follow through.

Becoming more evolved is important for more than your own sake. In a sense, your personal health is tied to the health and evolvement of the species. We share this world together. We all draw equally on the universal force. Thus, one of our purposes on earth is to realize that we exist as one: no person can stand alone and be healthy. In an evolved society, we would treat one another as we best treat ourselves, with respect, concern, and consideration. We would exhibit a higher degree of control over our thought patterns. We would care more what others think of us, because the negative thoughts we create in others are socially harmful to each and every one of us.

In an evolved society, we would also respect the earth itself, knowing that our welfare derives from the health of that earth, for the energy in nature is the energy in us.

I will make one last prediction. Humankind is torn between two impulses. One of these is to evolve, the other is to destroy. If civilization doesn't kill us off with its weaponry and pollution, we will indeed reach that state of higher evolvement. Our vibration rate will increase, and more and more of us will be sensitive to the life force. Our general health, both physical and mental, will improve. People will become increasingly thoughtful and at ease with their essential natures. Small changes are already happening. But the only way to ensure that larger changes occur is by taking care of yourself—physically, mentally, spiritually. Every act of consideration you take toward your own well-being is a healthy act for all of humankind.

8

Exercises

Over the past ten years I have developed with my friend and fellow osteopath, Dr. Richard Koss, a set of exercises designed to augment the life force.

These exercises were originally created for use after an osteopathic treatment, but they can be of benefit on their own, for they seem to make a great many people feel better. Often parents will complain about their own bad backs while I'm treating their child, and I'll show them the exercise for stretching out the bottom of the spine, for instance. The next time they bring the child in, they always tell me how good they feel since they began practicing the exercise.

Unfortunately, it's too difficult to perform osteopathic manipulation on yourself. These exercises are the closest approximation of it we have been able to create for stimulating the life force on your own. They may seem straightforward and simple, but they can have a profound effect. Doing them daily and properly will help you experience better health and increased vitality.

EXERCISE 1

Stand with your feet spread a shoulder-width apart and extend your arms out to your sides, approximately at shoulder height. Your left palm should face upward, and your right should face downward. (Holding the left palm faceup tightens the body, helping to stretch the muscles.)

Make sure that you take full, deep breaths.

If you can, try to stand in this position for a full ten minutes. (I myself have never made it past eight.) The longer you can do it, however, the better.

When you get to the point where you're too tired to hold your arms up any longer, still keeping them

straight, slowly raise them
above your head, without
allowing them to come forward. Then, lower them to
your sides.

Because many patients find
this exercise too demanding,
we've devised a variation: sit
on a couch and place your
arms along the back, also with
your left palm up and right
palm down, and sit still for
fifteen minutes.

This exercise puts a good
tension on the muscles in
and around the arms and
strengthens the back muscles.
If you're doing this correctly,
you should soon start to feel
the tissues in the shoulders
opening up, allowing your
respiration to expand.

EXERCISE 2

This exercise is called the regenerative breath, or piston
breath. (We had to simplify its name when we found
that children couldn't pronounce the word "regenerative.")

Sitting comfortably in a chair, breathe in and out
rapidly through the nostrils, imitating the motion of an

automobile piston going in and out. Take the breath in, blow it out right away; quickly take another one, let it out; and keep going, breathing in and out, in and out, in and out.

I usually ask patients to start with ten piston breaths, because that's all that many can do comfortably. When that becomes easy, we increase the number to twenty, and when twenty becomes easy, we go to forty, and so on to sixty, then eighty, and then one hundred. If you can, repeat another hundred.

This exercise may sound simple, but you might be surprised at how many people can't do it well. If you didn't get that full, first breath at childbirth, it will take you more time than you think to build up to a hundred.

By performing the piston-breath exercise, you should be able to regenerate every cell in your body—in other words, you can bring stagnated cells that haven't been functioning well back into normal activity.

EXERCISE 3

For the next exercise, you must lie down on the floor and stretch out your arms, with the left palm facing up and the right facing down, as in the first exercise. Then, without trying to bring the knee or the foot up to the head, swing one leg over to the opposite side of your body, crossing leg over leg. Let the leg come to rest where it wants. Simply position it where you're comfortable, and then lie still for five minutes. When the time is up, repeat the exercise using the opposite leg for five more minutes.

This exercise stretches the muscles in the pelvis and is particularly useful for women who've just given birth, or for anyone whose back has been aching.

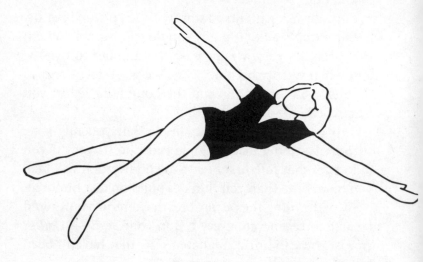

EXERCISE 4

Here is a good stretch to help keep the lower part of the back pliable.

Sit in an upright chair with your thighs parallel to the floor and the lower part of your legs perpendicular to the floor. Bend over, placing your elbows on the inside of your knees and your hands between your feet; turn your palms away from each other, tuck your fingers under the arch of each foot and your thumb over the top of the foot. Let your spine fully stretch in this position.

Breathe slowly and fully for five minutes. Do this once a day and you'll notice that walking is much eas-

ier, you can stand up straighter, and your back feels lighter.

If you're limber enough to prefer doing this standing up, that's okay. If, however, you've been feeling pain in your sciatic nerve, omit this exercise, for it could worsen the pain.

EXERCISE 5

Stand against a wall so that your heels, lower back, shoulder blades, and the back of your head touch the wall. Then, raise your arms straight out in front of you, letting your thumbs touch each other. As slowly as possible, raise your arms straight above your head until you finally touch the wall. Then, lower your arms out and down to your sides. Again, remember to breathe slowly and fully. Do this two times, once a day.

This exercise helps pull the rib cage into its normal position, frees up the diaphragm, and stretches the muscles all the way from the pelvis to the root of the skull.

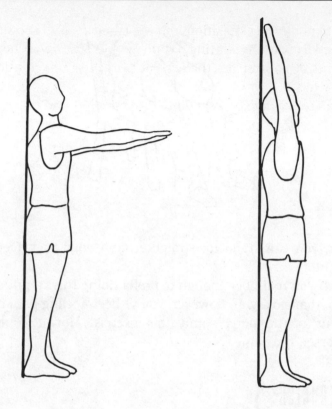

EXERCISE 6

These shoulder rolls were developed for office workers stuck at a desk in front of a computer all day.

Sit in a chair with your back straight and both feet on the floor. Next, bend your elbows in front of you and let your fingertips rest on the tops of your shoulders. Breathing slowly and fully, as always, on the inhalation lift your elbows toward the ceiling and lower your head.

Then, on the exhalation, roll the elbows out to the side and back to the starting position while lifting your head back. This stretches the head and breaks up the tension pattern.

Try this five times, two to three times a day.

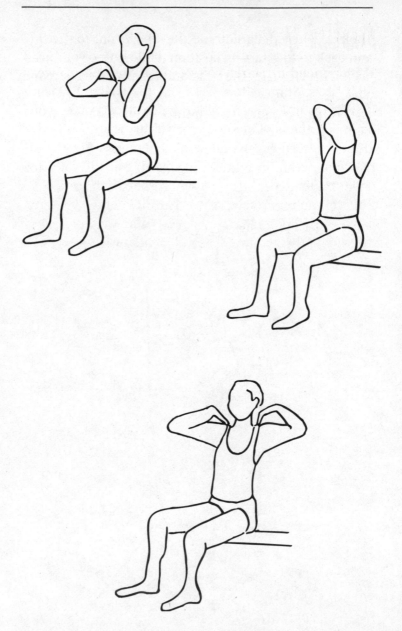

EXERCISE 7

I recommend this stretch mostly for women who wear high heels. Stand a few feet from the wall and, facing it with your feet a shoulder-width apart, place your palms on the wall at shoulder height. Then bend your knees as much as possible while keeping your heels on the floor. While the knees are bent, breathe fully for one minute. Repeat this five times, once a day.

Here you're stretching the Achilles tendon, which, particularly in females, shortens due to high heels. Stretching this tendon helps you walk properly.

EXERCISE 8

This last exercise I often give to patients who develop a stiff neck. Place your hands behind your head and, keeping your head absolutely straight in place, simultaneously press your head against your hands and your hands against your head. Do this for as long as you wish.

We call this the push-and-pull exercise, as you push the head forward with the hands and use the head to resist that push. This stretches the muscles in the neck area and frees up circulation there, as well as in the brain.

If you've just done these exercises, you've stretched and freed up major parts of the body in approximately half an hour. These are all the exercises necessary to get the life force flowing freely through your body. Do them carefully, and your health should improve.

9

Notes for Further Thinking and Reading

"Osteopathy to me is a very sacred science. It is sacred because it is a healing power through all nature."

—ANDREW TAYLOR STILL

Over the years innumerable people have influenced my professional work and my personal thinking. I would like to mention a special few of them and recommend several books for those readers interested in learning more about some of the ideas presented in this book.

Dr. Andrew Taylor Still, the founder of osteopathy, inspired me greatly while I was in school and continues to do so to this day. The more experience I accumulate as an osteopath, the more I find I agree with his body of thought. With his wisdom and tenacity, Dr. Still has left the American public a great bequest. Very few people possess the kind of courage he needed to persevere in the face of the medical establishment's massive censure of osteopathy. Whenever a problem arrises that I don't feel capable of handling, I turn to Dr. Still's *Philosophy and Mechanical Principles of Osteopathy*, published in 1902, and reread his words. Almost always, I find an answer within them.

Dr. Still did not investigate life as if through a magnifying glass, bringing matter within a fixed field of vision. He had a much broader concept of life. He studied it through the equivalent of minimizing glasses, bringing within his field of vision matter that is usually beyond the reach of the human eye. His goal was understanding the cohesion of phenomena, rather than the analysis of matter.

Readers interested in learning more about Dr. Still himself might want to look at *The Frontier Doctor: Medical Pioneer* (The Thomas Jefferson University Press, 1991), written by his grandson, Dr. Charles Still, Jr.

Dr. William Sutherland, a Minnesota osteopath who studied under Dr. Still, developed what is know as the theory of craniosacral motion, which involves the movement of the skull bones, the motility of its membranes, and their connection to respiration. As I mentioned earlier, mainstream science once routinely mocked the notion that the skull bones could move, but recent research has proven that Dr. Sutherland was correct.

I consider the most important day of my life to have been when I had the opportunity in the late 1940s to sit in Dr. Sutherland's classroom at the Des Moines College of Osteopathy, where I was jolted from my customary channels of thought by the sheer force of his teachings.

Dr. Sutherland expressed many of his ideas through symbols. For instance, in one of his classes he drew on the blackboard a picture of a three-story house floating upon the ocean. The best explanation of this image is found in the book *A Model of the Universe*, by P. D. Ouspensky, in which the author describes the ocean as a body of water in which the mind of nature operates as an energy field within the atmosphere. The floating house represents the various human minds. That part of the house submerged in the water is the instinctive mind. The first floor is the subconscious mind, the second floor the intellectual mind, and the third floor the spiritual mind. Altogether, the picture expresses the constant rhythmic interchange that takes place between the mind of nature and the human mind.

Dr. Sutherland's picture might also be expressed in terms of equilibrium. All living bodies are energy systems, which strive to maintain themselves in a state of dynamic equilibrium. When this dynamic equilibrium becomes upset, the organism feels a need or a hunger. The hunger arouses the

organism to modify its existing pattern, so a rees-
tablishment of the equilibrium can take place.

Dr. Sutherland never abandoned his view that
in order to understand the whole, whether of life
or of man, one must analyze the elements of which
it was constructed—consistent with the Newtonian theory that the whole is the sum of its parts.
Dr. Sutherland took this idea a step further. He believed the characteristics of the whole are derived
not only from the properties of its component
parts, but from their interaction with one another.
It isn't possible to understand any object in isola-
tion from the surroundings with which it interacts.
Unfortunately, when Dr. Sutherland introduced
this idea, it was neither appreciated nor accepted.

But Dr. Sutherland's insights again proved pre-
scient, because later amendments to Newtonian
laws of physics confirmed what he had been saying all along. For Newtonian theory breaks down
at the level of subatomic particles. There we find
not individual matter but an oscillating field and
waves of rhythm. At its essence everything dis-
solves into pure rhythm. Everything vibrates with
the life force.

Dr. Sutherland was a quiet man whose radiance
spoke of a tremendous vitality of spirit. In his eyes
flickered a constant, subtle, inspiring light. When
his vision took you in and those eyes narrowed,
you could feel that he was gazing not at your physical body, but at your inner being.

*　*　*

Walter Russell was a master of five different arts—
architecture, sculpture, painting, music, and litera-
ture—and was, I believe, one of the world's great
thinkers. Taken out of school when he was ten
years old and put to work, he was a totally self-
educated person. I often turn to his writings also
when I'm unable to resolve a problem.

Russell was once asked how he acquired his scientific knowledge. He replied: "I always looked for
the Cause behind things and didn't fritter away my
time analyzing Effect. All knowledge exists as
Cause. It is simple. It is limited to Light of Mind
and the electric wave of motion which records
God's thinking in matter."

He was also once asked to define reality. He replied:

> Is the product of mind the reality, or is the
> thought which causes the product the reality?
> We all look in the direction of our product,
> thinking mistakenly that that thing which we
> created is the real thing. The real substance of
> any product is not in the product at all, but is
> only in the thought behind the product. The
> thought is never created. The thought belongs
> to the thinker and to other thinkers who are
> capable of interpreting the symbolic form.
>
> As a general principle, you can see how that
> applies to everything in life, whether you are
> a salesman, a doctor, an artist, or a business-
> man. Therefore, to get back into the real sub-

stance of things, you must get back into the Thought World. Until one knows that the thought energy is the cause which is back of all things, and the product only the effect. If he is tied to the effect and is limited by it, he belongs to the world of imitation and that world only.

It was through Russell that I was able to confirm my belief in a universal source. He also brought my attention to the Law of Balance Interchange, or what I call the law of give and regive, and it underlies all of my work.

Those interested in Russell's work might want to read his book, *A New Concept of the Universe* (University of Science and Philosophy, 1989). An excellent biography of him is *The Man Who Tapped the Secrets of the Universe*, by Glenn Clark, from the same publisher.

I first read about Yale professor Harold Burr's experiments with a voltmeter and nature in 1939. What he found corresponded directly with what Dr. Still, Dr. Sutherland, and Walter Russell each asserted: the life force penetrates all living things. Dr. Burr's book is called *Blueprint for Immortality: The Electric Pattern of Life* (Redwood Burn Ltd., 1977).

Dr. Valerie V. Hunt's work confirms the early work on the life force. Dr. Hunt, who was a physiologist at the University of California at Los

Angeles, has been doing research in the field of bioenergetics for many years. Her findings indicate that the whole body is an electromagnetic field. Because few instruments can pick up these energies, Dr. Hunt is developing more sensitive tools to detect them. Her book is *The Infinite Mind: Science of Human Vibrations* (Malibu Publishing Co., 1995).

Another scientist whose work has influenced me greatly was Marcel Vogel, formerly a senior research scientist at IBM. An international authority on luminescence and a leading figure in the development of fluorescent lights, he later devoted his research time to the science of breath and to the field called transformational medicine. Vogel believed, as I do, that thoughts are energy. They have forms in space. When we think, an energy emanates from our bodies with a distinct pattern, and that energy comes out through the breath.

Once more I'd like to mention the work of Wilhelm Reich, the Austrian-born American psychoanalyst, biophysicist, and a founder of the New School for Social Research in New York City. From Reich I learned a great deal about how the emotions act upon the human body. Reich observed that the inhibition of respiration had a direct connection to the inhibition of feelings. He believed that the respiratory disturbances in emotionally unstable individuals were the result of abdominal tension. He described how this tension produced shallow breathing and how, in fright, one holds one's breath by clenching the abdominal muscles.

Through the Austrian actor F. Matthias Alexander, I learned a great deal about conscious control of the human body's psychophysical makeup. His Alexander Technique teaches new ways to move that can improve posture, balance, and coordination, all of which can relieve tension and pain. He developed the technique after he lost his voice and was unable to get any help from traditional medicine. After experimenting on himself, he discovered that the correct positioning of his head upon his neck was vital to good vocal function. Alexander wrote two books: *Man's Supreme Inheritance* and *The Universal One.*

For readers interested in learning more about human electrical properties, I recommend *The Body Electric,* by Robert O. Becker, M.D. (William Morrow, 1985). Dr. Becker, who was an orthopedic surgeon at a VA hospital in Syracuse, New York, and a professor at the Upstate Medical Center, conducted research similar to Dr. Burr's, using more modern instruments, and came up with results that advanced the work further. Another good book is John Diamond's *Life Energy* (Dodd Mead, 1985), which discusses the life energy and its connection to the thymus gland. I also recommend *The Nuclear Evolution: The Discovery of the Rainbow Body,* by Christopher Hill (University of the Trees Press, 1968), which is a wonderful discussion of many of the topics covered in this book.

Finally, several friends and peers contributed to this book in more ways than they may realize.

These include my loyal secretary of eighteen years, Madeline Rathjen, as well as Dr. Zachary Comeaux, Dr. and Mrs. Anthony Chila, Dr. Carol Dawson, Dr. Paula Eschtruth, Dr. Richard Koss, Dr. Sarah Sexton, and Dr. William Stager. I also want to thank my editor at Pocket Books, Tom Spain, as well as my agent, Richard Pine.

For more information about osteopathy, and a listing of osteopaths near you, contact:

American Academy of Osteopathy
3500 DePauw Boulevard, Suite 1080
Indianapolis, Indiana 46268
(317) 879-1881